PHANTOMS OF THE HIGH SEAS

PHANTOMS OF THE HIGH SEAS

by

Philip MacDougall

REED

By the same author

Mysteries on the High Seas
Royal Dockyards

First published in Australia by

Reed Books Pty Ltd
3/470 Sydney Road, Balgowlah NSW 2093

ISBN 0 7301 0313 7

By arrangement with
David & Charles plc
Brunel House
Newton Abbot, Devon, England

Set and printed for David & Charles
by Redwood Press Ltd, Pegasus Way,
Bowerhill Industrial Estate,
Melksham, Wilts.

Contents

Introduction & Acknowledgements		6
1	Forewarned	11
2	Yo, Ho, Oh . . . !	24
3	The Pilot of the *Pinta*	35
4	The Ghost of the *Great Eastern*	41
5	The Transparent Lady. A True Ghost Story?	54
6	A Malevolent Ghost?	63
7	Phantom Ships	78
8	The *Ellen Austin* Mystery	94
9	The Headless Mate	99
10	The Legend of the Damned	103
11	The Ghost of the *Eurydice*	121
12	Smuggling Haunts	130
13	Into the Teeth of Death	143
14	The Haunted Dockyard and other Naval Ghosts	163
	Bibliography	181
	Notes and Sources	183
	Index	191

Introduction

Although a great number of books have been written about ghosts and other psychic phenomena, surprisingly few have been directed towards the task of examining these same unusual occurrences when they have taken place somewhere on the world's oceans. This, indeed, is most surprising. Over the centuries there have been an amazing number of inexplicable incidents that have involved seagoing ships and their crews and undoubtedly, the vast majority have some form of connection with the supernatural. It is with the intention of correcting this deficiency that this book has been written.

I have taken a deliberately broad approach to the subject. Rather than concentrating entirely upon ghosts, doppelgangers and poltergeists, I have also taken a look at other aspects of the supernatural. In particular this is the case with the opening chapter. Here, with just a few words that might whet the appetite, I have concentrated upon a number of reports in which individuals are supposed to have received strong psychic warnings as to the fate of the *Titanic* on her ill-fated maiden voyage. A number of those who received these warnings had actually booked passage on the ship, with some of them choosing to cancel. This partly explains why the *Titanic*, upon leaving Southampton, had a number of empty berths.

I have been particularly concerned to include only incidents that could be fully verified. This, in itself, makes the present book different from most other accounts that relate to the supernatural and the maritime world. Several previous writers have been inclined to accept a number of bizarre and extreme assertions without the slightest hesitation. In this book, I have avoided such trusting faith in every dubious claim, unprepared to admit it as definite evidence as to the existence of a supernatural world. The outcome is that a number of widely accepted marine ghost stories have been rejected, while I have felt inclined to cast doubt upon others. Despite this, I feel that I am left with material that is sufficient to excite the appetite.

To assure the reader as to the accuracy, or reasons for doubting a given account, I have presented a full list of sources together with a discussion as to their veracity. Sometimes this appears in the text, but more often it is to be found in the additional notes at the end of the book. This is an approach that has been rarely adopted by previous writers on this subject. While I, personally, would not claim to be an out and out believer in the world of supernature I feel, nevertheless, that there are a number of incidents which cannot easily be explained. Frequently, those who have seen ghosts or have been exposed to other psychic phenomena, are men and women whose honesty and critical capacities would appear to be beyond reproach. Amongst those whose names are included in this book are various naval captains and masters of merchant ships, not usually noted for having a fanciful turn of mind, together with members of several professional bodies and a future king of Great Britain. All in all, they are witnesses of the very highest calibre!

Now, as to the matter of what may actually have been seen. The ghostly form of a once departed sailor or long deceased smuggler may certainly be the apparition of his or her spirit. But such a conclusion can hardly be true when it comes to the sighting of a ghost ship: a monstrous timber or metal structure. If nothing else, such manufactured monsters have no spirit. Instead, if I may digress a moment, I feel that a more plausible explanation is that such a vision is merely a projection of the mind – either that of the witness or somebody associated with the episode that has been recreated.

The result, quite naturally, is the re-appearance of a long lost vessel which might have been wrecked in that same area of water. Such an idea can be used to explain the occasional appearance of the ghost ship *Eurydice* off the Isle of Wight together with other similar vessels associated with the Goodwin Sands.

Author Lyall Watson, takes this particular theme a good deal further. In his book, *Supernature*, he suggests that such a projection of the mind could well be the real reason why ghosts are always reported as fully clothed. Watson further declares that he is prepared 'in principle' to accept the possible existence of 'an astral body', but cannot bring himself to accept 'astral shoes, shirts and hats'. As he goes on to conclude, 'the fact that people see ghosts as they or somebody else remembers them, fully dressed in period costume, seems to indicate that the visions are part of a mental process.'

It is not, however, my intention to discuss this particular aspect of the supernature debate. I mention it merely as a possible alternative explanation to the existence of the classic ghost. In fact, the purpose of this book is not to enter into this discussion, but simply to report events that have been seen, heard or predicted. I mention thought projection only in passing, leaving it to the reader to determine what might be behind the various peculiar events that appear in the pages of this book. Hopefully, each chapter will be found to be both entertaining and thought provoking. That, quite simply, is the purpose of this book.

In putting together this collection of happenings I would like to thank a number of individuals. First and foremost are those who replied to my requests for information concerning personal experiences of the supernatural intermingling itself with the seagoing world. In particular, I wish to mention Roy Davies, Mrs M. A. Jarvis (former member of the WRNS), Mrs E. Maleham, Stuart Rockett (formerly of HMS *Mercury*) and Arthur Samuel.

In addition I received help from the staff in a number of

libraries (especially the town libraries of Birkenhead, Pembroke, Plymouth, Portsmouth and Rochester) together with the staff and volunteers of the Block Island Historical Society (Block Island U.S.A.), British Library Newspaper Library (Colindale), Carisbrooke Castle Museum (Isle of Wight), The Maritime Museum (Bembridge), Public Record Office (Kew), Rhode Island Historical Society (Providence), Royal Naval College library (Greenwich), Royal Naval Museum (Portsmouth), the Society for Psychical Research (London) and the United States Naval Institute (Annapolis). In all cases, those involved in answering my numerous queries deserve a full acknowledgement of my gratitude.

The last moments of HMS *Eurydice* as later described to a journalist by one of only two survivors. Her spectre has been seen off the Isle of Wight

The last moments of the *Titanic*. Amongst those on board the vessel at the time of her loss were a number of individuals who appear to have been clearly forewarned of the disaster. Unfortunately for them they failed to act upon these premonitions.

1

Forewarned

On 14 April 1910 the SS *Titanic*, then the world's largest passenger liner, struck an iceberg during her maiden voyage. Eventually disappearing into the near-freezing depths of the North Atlantic, she claimed the lives of almost 1,500 passengers and crew. The sheer enormity of this sudden and unexpected tragedy has resulted in the *Titanic* being considered the gauge by which all subsequent maritime disasters are measured.

At the time of her loss, the *Titanic* carried a total of 1320 passengers, (337 first class, 271 second class and 712 third class), together with a crew of just over 900. Should various newspaper reports be accepted as fact, then it is clear that a great many of these passengers and crew were convinced that the vessel was doomed even before she left her home port of Southampton.

Strange as it may seem, many of those boarding the *Titanic* had received a forwarning of the coming disaster. The majority seem to have ignored these warnings, accepting the popular opinion that this latest technological wonder was unsinkable. Others did take some form of action. In some cases this took the form of a warning to friends and relatives that they might never see them again while others simply put their affairs in order before leaving. Additionally, of course, a number of those who were subject to these premonitions changed their minds about boarding the ship. In fact, it must be counted as one of the reasons why the *Titanic*, on that much publicised voyage, sailed partially empty. In point of fact, she had accommodation for a further eight hundred or more passengers.

This belief in the ship being doomed, even before she sailed, must rate among the most peculiar episodes of maritime history. After all, she was one of the largest, most comfortable and technically efficient liners ever to attempt a crossing of the Atlantic. Having a displacement of 60,000 tons, she was nearly a sixth of a mile in length (882.5 ft) while her height was equal to that of an eleven storey building. As for her engines, these were capable of developing power in excess of 50,000 hp and sufficient to give the vessel a maximum speed of 25 knots. Considered the safest vessel afloat, her security was ensured by a double bottom and sixteen watertight compartments. Yet, despite this wealth of sophistication, hundreds of ordinary people were convinced that the *Titanic* would never reach America!

As for proof of these psychic forewarnings it is only necessary to turn to the pages of various contemporary newspapers. In reporting the tragedy, many of them carried interviews with those who had, in some way, come into contact with the *Titanic*. Without prompting, and unknown to each other, a surprisingly large number mention inexplicable fears that led them to believe that the vessel was doomed.

It is the local papers in the ship's home port of Southampton that provide the largest concentration of such reports. Because many of the crew were natives of this particular town, local journalists were able to visit a number of bereaved families. In addition, they also came upon a number of individuals who were due to have joined the *Titanic* but chose not to do so. Two items that appeared in the *Southampton Times* are of particular interest. The first relates to an interview carried out on the doorstep of a small terraced house in Andersons Road:

> Mrs Burrows was to be seen there and she said,
> 'My son Harry goes to sea, and he had stayed home

for a month in the expectation of getting engaged on the *Titanic*. He went down to the docks to sign on, but at the last moment changed his mind and came away, for which we are very thankful. I can't explain why he changed his mind, some sort of feeling came over him, he told me.' [*Southampton Times and Hampshire Express*, 20 April 1912]

The second of two reports from the *Southampton Times* proves even more intriguing:

Inquiries in Chantry Road led to the discovery that in one house there resided four men, all of whom signed to sail on the *Titanic*, but arrived at the quay side too late to get on board. They were the three brothers Slade and another named Penney. They left home together to go to the ship, but when they arrived, the gangway had been removed, and they were told they could go home again. Mrs Slade was seen by our representative, and her first words were, 'What a good job they missed their ship! I have thanked God for it ever since.' 'How did they miss the boat?' was asked. 'I can't tell you exactly, but they left home in good time. Somehow or other my boys did not seem very keen on going in the ship. You may not believe in dreams, but I am telling you the truth when I say that one of my boys had a dream about the boat the night before sailing day, and he afterwards said that he had a dread of her. I know they were not very keen on going, but nevertheless they went down. The engineer called to them to get on board, but for some reason or other they didn't go.' [*Southampton Times and Hampshire Express*, 20 April 1912]

A second Southampton newspaper, the *Hampshire Independent*, also carried a number of similar reports. One of these concerned members of the Ward family:

'Please I've got a cable from my dad. He's saved'.

These were the words of little Jackie Ward, who rushed into our office yesterday morning, his face beaming with delight. He told us that his father was making his first trip as a steward in the employ of the White Star Company, having previously sailed on American boats. He is an Australian, as is also Mrs. Ward, who needless to say, was over-joyed at the news of her husband's safety. This is the sixth time that Mr. Ward has been wrecked. On one occasion he was picked up after being two days in an open boat under tropical skies. Mrs. Ward waited for hours outside the White Star offices on Monday and Tuesday, but gave up all hope on Wednesday, and 'broke down' as Jackie said. Her hopes were revived when she received a letter from her husband's mother, 14,000 miles away in Australia, saying that her son had gone through so many perils that she had no fears for his safety. Jackie, too, was full of hope and regularly prayed that his father would be rescued. A re-markable thing was that he told his father not to go 'as the ship was going to roll over'. Since the disas-ter, the little lad told us, he had dreamed three times in succession that he and his father and mother went to the 'pictures' which fact convinced him that no harm would come to his father.'.
[*Hampshire Independent*, 20 April 1912]

In addition, the *Hampshire Independent* carried two fur-ther reports relating to those who may well have had premo-nitions of the forthcoming tragedy. Indeed, one of them went so far as to desert the ship at Queenstown in Southern Ire-land, (better known to-day as Cobh), the *Titanic*'s last port of call before heading out into the Atlantic:

One man who sailed from Southampton with grave, but undefinable misgivings, left the boat at Queenstown. Another, a steward who lived in the Shirley district told his wife before his departure, that he wished he had never 'signed on'. [*Hampshire Independent*, 20 April 1912]

A second British city that was closely connected with the *Titanic* was Belfast. It was here, at the Harland & Wolff shipyard, that she was launched on 31 May 1911. Over the following months the thousands of workers involved in her construction, together with their families and friends, would have taken a close interest in the vessel's progress. The resulting tragedy, which came as a severe shock to the Belfast community, was treated in great detail by each of the local newspapers. Again, there were numerous references to those who appear to have received some form of psychic forewarning. The *Belfast Evening Telegraph* provides the first of two examples:

> Amongst the many weird stories of the *Titanic*, perhaps the most remarkable is that of the restaurant staff. No fewer than ten cousins of the manager, Mr. L. Gatti – who is reported missing – were engaged in preparing food for the ship. Their fate is unknown, but it was foreseen by the wife of Mr. Gatti, whose home was at Southampton.
>
> The shadow of danger disturbed her sleep on the night the ship went down. She had a strange presentiment of danger and could not rest.
> In the morning her presentiment had such an effect on her that, on Monday, she travelled to London and stayed with her sister.
> But her restlessness pursued her until the news of the disaster arrived. [*Belfast Evening Telegraph*, 18 April 1912]

Some weeks after that particular report, the *Belfast Newsletter* carried this story which is headed as 'Wexford Man's Dream:

> Mr Patrick O'Keeffe, of Spring Garden Alley, Waterford, who was saved from the *Titanic*, has

written a letter to his father in which he states that the night before he sailed from Queenstown he dreamt the *Titanic* was going down. [*Belfast News-letter*, 7 May 1912]

However, such reports of psychic forewarning were not simply restricted to those towns in some way specially connected with the *Titanic*. Consider this range of examples drawn from a number of different regional papers published in the weeks immediately following the loss of the *Titanic*. *The New York Tribune* carried this particular story collected from Hemingford, Nebraska:

> Because she dreamed she saw the *Titanic* sinking, Mrs. B. O. Shepherd of Hemingford, sent word to her husband in England to cancel his reservation on that steamer and to return on another boat. The fact that he did so probably saved his life.
>
> The dream took place two months ago, Mrs. Shepherd first wrote to her husband asking him not to take the *Titanic* home. She then sent a cable message to him to the same effect. Although he had already taken passage on that steamer, Shepherd transferred to another White Star boat. [*New York Tribune*, 22 April, 1912]

The Washington Post gleaned this story from New York:

> The fallacy and infallibility of fortune tellers is not always to be relied on said one of the officers of the steamship *George Washington*, when a matter of superstitions, vague fears and forebodings was brought up.
>
> I have been going to sea for a great many years, and in the natural course of things a lot of the tradition of the sea have been rubbed in. There is one incident in particular that was strange. Last year in Bremerhaven my wife and I with our two daughters went to the fair – a cattle fair it was – and the outlying grounds were filled with a gypsy camp.

For the fun of the thing we decided to have the future read. Oh, so old a crone. She was 80 if a day, and as her dim eyes peered into the hollow of my palm I could not help laughing.

Shaking with palsy, she looked up, and there was a peculiar expression in her wavering stare.

'You may laugh,' she quavered. 'They always do laugh, but on the sea lies your work, and next year the greatest ship in the world will sink – sink – sink!'

And still I laughed.

She thrust my hand aside and began to cry. 'I have told you too much! Sadness – death – sinking – sinking!'

My wife and I left the crazy quilt tent – still laughing.' [*Washington Post*, 21 April 1912]

Several newspapers published in North America also carried references to reported fears of Major Archibald Butt, a military aide to President Taft who was among the 1,500 who died on that fateful night in April:

> A mysterious warning that he would meet death on his trip abroad came to Major Archibald Butt before he left Washington six weeks ago when the major determined on a European trip to regain his health. A premonition that he might not return alive caused him to make his will. He called in a lawyer and closed his affairs. [*Montreal Star*, 17 April 1912]

Returning to the British Isles, this intriguing report came from the tiny Irish village of Athenry:

> A strange report of a mother's dream in connection with the *Titanic* disaster comes from Athenry, where a young farmer had determined to emigrate, and had, in fact, made arrangements for the booking of his passage on the ill-fated *Titanic*. His mother, however, dreamed three nights in suc-

cession that the boat upon which her son was to travel had gone down and in her vision she states she saw the vessel sinking in mid-ocean with all on board. So deep an impression did the dream make upon her that she pleaded with her son to remain at home and ultimately succeeded in keeping him. Four days after the liner on which he was to sail had left Queenstown, her remarkable dream had been in part, at least, fulfilled. [*The Cork Examiner*, 2 May 1912]

Finally, in case there is a temptation to believe that each and every cancelled passage came about as the result of a premonition, it is useful to refer to this more down to earth offering from Margate in Kent. It concerns Norman Craig, the Member of Parliament for that particular constituency:

A wonderful piece of luck appears to have favoured the MP for Thanet. Mr Craig had indeed booked his passage and until the day before Good Friday had intended to sail for New York in the newest leviathan. Intuition without any presentiment suggested he would be better advised to remain at home during the Home Rule debate in the House of Commons and the passage was cancelled. [*Isle of Thanet Gazette*, 20 April 1912]

Another of those lost in this great tragedy was a certain W. T. Stead, a well known journalist who edited the periodical *Review of Reviews*, and who had a particular interest in spiritualism. Indeed, Stead himself claimed the ability to communicate with the 'other world' through the use of automatic writing.

As part of his interest in spiritualism, Stead had made a point of visiting a large number of mediums, palm readers and others who claimed the ability to view the future. During the course of his visits, many of these clairvoyants had made predictions about Stead's future, several of them specifically referring to how his life would eventually end. Admittedly, several of their predictions were contradictory, but a number of them (perhaps the majority) were extremely close to the truth. Indeed, if Stead had but realised it, he was in fact warned of the impending disaster.

One of the earliest of these predictions was made in January 1892 when a palm reader clearly indicated that he would die during the year 1912. A previous clairvoyant had, so it should be pointed out, indicated that Stead's death would come in 1924. However, even given this conflict of information, the fact that one of these two clairvoyants should accurately predict the year of his demise is, in itself, quite remarkable.

Of the various clairvoyants that Stead chose to visit, there is a remarkable similarity in at least one of their predictions. On numerous occasions, Stead was informed that he would be threatened by water, with one of them going as far as to associate this with a huge passenger liner. The most accurate of these predictions came in May 1911. While attending a seance held in Detroit, the spirit of a native American informed him that he would die after one further crossing of the Atlantic. This is exactly what happened!

Stead, for his own part, seemed remarkably unaffected by these warnings. Certainly he does not appear to have had any qualms upon boarding the *Titanic*. During the first day of his voyage he penned a letter, subsequently posted from Queenstown. Written to a close friend, it declared the ship to be 'as firm as a rock' and added that he felt able to work better on board 'for there are no telephones to worry me, and no callers.'

Another interesting facet of W. T. Stead's connection with the *Titanic* are the themes of two stories he wrote towards the end of the nineteenth century. The first of these, published in *The Pall Mall Gazette* in 1886, concerns the sinking of an ocean liner and describes an excessive number of lives being lost because the vessel had an inadequate number of lifeboats. That W. T. Stead and many others were to lose their lives was directly related to the same problem. The *Titanic* had only twenty lifeboats sufficient for only about half the total number of passengers carried by the vessel on that maiden voyage.

The second of Stead's two stories was entitled 'From the Old World to the New', published in the Christmas 1892 edition of the *Review of Reviews*. This included an account of a passenger liner coming to the rescue of a few survivors from another vessel that had struck an iceberg. Although a work of fiction this story did contain some factual background and remarkably, the rescuing liner, apart from being owned by the White Star Company, was captained by no less a person than Edward Smith. In later years this same Captain Smith commanded the *Titanic* during her maiden voyage and went down with his ship.

Having referred to W. T. Stead's two fictional and almost prescient accounts concerning transatlantic liners it would seem appropriate to refer to the novel *Futility*, written by Morgan Robertson and published in 1898. It too centres upon icebergs and passenger liners. Although Morgan Robertson himself did not board the *Titanic*, the similarity of his story with events that occurred in April 1912 suggests that he, too, might have been forewarned of the coming tragedy.

To begin with, it is impossible to ignore the similarity of names, with Morgan giving his fictional vessel the name *Titan*. But this was only the beginning of a vast number of similarities between Morgan's fictional ship and the real *Titanic*.

Of particular importance was the fact that both ships were registered under the British flag but were actually American owned. Many British readers may, in fact, he surprised to learn this particular fact relating to the *Titanic*. Since 1902, controlling interest in the White Star Company had been in the hands of American shipping magnate, J. P. Morgan. As regards the vessels themselves, both were the largest of their day, with Robertson giving his *Titan* a displacement of 70,000 tons and a length of 800 ft the *Titanic*, as already mentioned, had a displacement of 60,000 tons and was of 882 ft. Both ships had a maximum passenger and crew capacity of 3000 and a possible top speed of 25 knots. In addition, both vessels were powered by triple expansion engines with the *Titan* having similar watertight bulkheads to those of the *Titanic*. Finally, both ships were of steel construction.

With the *Titan* departing from New York and the *Titanic* from Southampton, both vessels embarked upon their respective trans-Atlantic voyages during the month of April. Travelling at close on their maximum speeds for most of the voyage, the two vessels encountered their respective life destroying icebergs in the North Atlantic and at points that were no more than a hundred or so miles distant from one another. As a result, the *Titan* hit the immovable object at a speed of 25 knots and the *Titanic* at a speed of 22.5 knots. In both cases, the end result was the piercing of an extensive underwater area on the starboard side of the hull. So extensive was the damage that a number of watertight compartments were breached with both vessels only in a position to remain afloat for a few hours. As in Stead's earlier story involving the White Star liner *Majestic*, the number of lives lost from both the fictional *Titan* and the very real *Titanic* were considerably inflated due to a simple shortage of lifeboats. Robertson's *Titan* had been equipped with 24 lifeboats but this was sufficient for only 500 of the 3000 that she carried.

Considerable discussion has been directed towards the subject matter of Robertson's book. It is an interesting debating point as to whether *Futility* is the product of coincidence or genuine psychic forewarning. Although the similarity between the *Titan* and *Titanic* are certainly rather surprising, the rest of the book has little connection with real life events. In fact the story line is rather tedious involving an unlikely meeting on the decks of the *Titan* between two former friends. Lacking sound characterization and depth, the book has little to offer a modern day reader other than its similarity to events that took place 14 years after its publication.

Almost certainly, Robertson's book is a product of co-incidence. After all, if such coincidences did not exist, then the word itself would be non-existent or obsolete. Take, as just one example, his choice of *Titan* as the name of his fictional vessel. Given the fact that it was supposed to be the largest passenger liner in the world, the use of that particular name become almost compulsory. In fact, as the owners of the later White Star liner later decided, a name based on *Titan* or *Titanic* appears almost unavoidable.

However, the suggestion that Robertson's book was the product of coincidence does not necessarily extend to those numerous passengers, crew members, palm readers and spiritualists who all appear to have had certain fears relating to the *Titanic*. There are simply too many incidents of unrelated reports of forewarnings relating to the vessel. On both sides of the Atlantic, huge numbers of people were to claim that they had feared for the *Titanic*'s safety well before the beginning of that fateful maiden voyage.

If a large number of newspaper reports are to be believed many passengers booked on the *Titanic* were forewarned of disaster and refused to sail. Others ignored warnings. They included W. T. Stead (below left), a well known journalist with a strong interest in spiritualism and Major Archibald Butt (below right), a military aide to President Taft. Both were among the 1,500 passengers who died and both had received forewarnings.

2
Yo, ho, Oh . . . !

Can a deceased person have more than one ghost? This is the fascinating conundrum confronting those who take an interest in that infamous pirate, Captain William Kidd. According to tradition, his shadowy figure can be found lurking off New York's Long Island and in the by-ways of London. How can this be?

William Kidd, who is often considered to have been a highly successful and quite ruthless pirate, has a somewhat undeserved reputation. Indecisive and weak-minded, he drifted into piracy almost by accident. Certainly he was no born pirate, but in the early years of his life a respectable merchant trader and owner of the small sloop *Antegona*. Possibly as the result of greed, he appears to have fallen under the influence of a group of rather unscrupulous businessmen. They were able to convince him that money was to be made out of hunting pirates. In fact, they greatly exaggerated the rewards, convincing Kidd that he would acquire riches beyond measure. All he needed to do, so they told him, was to acquire a fast ship, a determined crew and a battery of guns.

According to these businessmen, any pirate ship attacked was bound to be loaded with priceless treasures. Once captured, all of this wealth would belong to Kidd and those who were helping finance him. Though somewhat immoral, if you remember that any property really belonged to those from whom it had originally been plundered, the plan was not actually illegal. Indeed, the English government was prepared to offer token support, seeing it as a means by which piracy on the high seas might be reduced.

At the time, so it should be indicated, open piracy was one of the greatest sea going hazards of the age. The previous 10 or 20 years had seen a massive increase in the numbers who had turned to this easy means of acquiring wealth, their activities going a long way to undermine international trade. Motivated as they were by greed, some of these pirates did at least show a degree of compassion for their victims. Sometimes they released crew members and passengers within sight of a nearby coastline, or allowed them to continue their journey once the ship in which they were travelling had been stripped of its wealth. Others however were quite pitiless and prepared to torture and maim those who opposed them, while taking any women as slaves or shackled concubines.

The contract which William Kidd eventually signed gave every appearance of being workable. However, it contained one extremely dubious clause. Should he be unsuccessful, then it was his responsibility to re-imburse all those, including that group of unscrupulous businessmen, who had chosen to put money into the venture. In other words, failure to return with at least £15,000 of captured cargo would result in the ruination of William Kidd himself.

The ship purchased for this novel anti-pirate campaign, and given the not inappropriate name of *Adventure*, was a hybrid type known as a galley frigate. Having the fore, main and mizzen masts of a typical fighting ship, she was also fitted with a set of long oars that were referred to as sweeps. Projecting from the lower deck, they could propel the vessel at a speed of three knots. Of course, they were only used when there was insufficient wind for her fore and aft rigged sails. However, in periods of calm they would give her a distinct advantage over any ship reliant only upon sail.

Although the main point of Kidd's voyage was to search out pirates, he was also given letters of marque, the special commision issued to private ships authorising them to capture enemy vessels. This privateering licence signed by King William III primarily referred to the French, the two nations having been in a more or less permanent period of hostility since 1688. Being in possession of these letters of marque, Kidd was operating as a privateer, legally on behalf of his country, whereas the pirates against whom he was also ordered to operate were outlaws to all nations. Concentrating his efforts in the Indian Ocean, Kidd spent six months searching these waters for pirate ships. However, he proved singularly unsuccessful. Not once did he encounter a pirate vessel. This was a situation which, if it continued, would result in Kidd having to refund his backers with a great deal more money than he actually possessed.

It was because of this trap into which he had freely entered that Kidd decided to embark upon his own piratical career. At first it was only a matter of liberally interpreting the wording of his royal warrant. To begin with therefore, Kidd only sought out vessels flying French colours, which he was entitled to do, but he subsequently attacked several neutrals which he was not entitled to do. Over the next few months as a result the amount of treasure carried on board the *Adventure* steadily mounted.

This lack of discernment with regard to the ships he attacked was eventually to prove his undoing. In November 1698 he captured the 500-ton *Quedah Merchant*. It was a circumstance which even the most generous interpretation of his royal warrant could not possibly cover, for the *Quedah Merchant* was an English ship. At his later trial, Kidd claimed that not only was this vessel failing to fly her national colours but that she had on board a pass signed by the Director-General of the Royal French East India Company. If this was so it was a mistake anyone could have made. However, Kidd chose to compound his original error by refusing to release the vessel once the captain had established her true nationality. Taking the vessel to St Mary's Island, off Madagascar, he proceeded to sell much of the cargo and convert the vessel for his own use.

Despite having committed several acts of piracy, Kidd appears to have been remarkably unconcerned about the dangers that he might now face upon returning to British territory. In the Summer of 1699, having replaced the *Adventure* and *Quedah Merchant* with a small sloop named *Antonio*, Kidd anchored in Long Island's Anchor Bay. This was not such an unusual place to have headed as might first appear. Lord Bellomont, then governor of New York, was one of Kidd's original backers. By approaching Bellomont and bringing with him such a vast amount of wealth, Kidd was trusting that the governor would overlook his various misdeeds and provide him with a pardon.

In reality, of course, it was an insane plan. Lord Bellomont, was unlikely to put his own head on the block even for those riches that Kidd was now offering. Instead, he helped organise Kidd's arrest, enticing him to leave Long Island and come to his residence in Boston. It was here, in the governor's house, that Kidd was eventually arrested.

Although Kidd had badly mis-read the situation, he was at least aware that there was a good chance of arrest. As a result, he decided that much of his captured treasure should be hidden. If all else failed, it might still be used as a bargaining counter. Before leaving for Boston, he made one important foray. This was to Gardiner's Island, which lies immediately to the north of Long Island. Here, close to Cherry Harbour beach, he buried a huge cache of gold bars, diamonds and valuable silks.

Following his arrest, Kidd was returned to England for trial. Facing five separate charges of piracy, he was accused of being an 'arch pirate, equally cruel, dreaded and hated both on the land and at sea'. With no witnesses to support him, and the French passes found on board the *Quedah Merchant* having mysteriously disappeared, Kidd had little chance of convincing the jury of his innocence. He was condemned to death and eventually met his fate on the edge of the River Thames, being hanged in Execution Dock at Wapping. His body was then painted with tar and encased in a metal harness so that it might be preserved and left to dangle from a special gibbet erected beside the busy river as a reminder to all who sailed to sea of the penalties for piracy, so they would not be tempted to take the same road as the infamous Captain Kidd.

Having desperately pleaded his innocence, it is hardly surprising that Captain Kidd's spirit should remain restless after such treatment. But which of the two apparitions, that off Long Island or the one to be found in the streets of London, is really his? Or is it truly possible that a man can have a spirit in two widely separated places?

The occasionally glimpsed apparition in London has been seen close to the point of execution, sometimes on the banks of the Thames and sometimes in nearby lanes. It is a ghost that most would surely avoid if they could, for Captain Kidd has a reputation that goes before him. In reality he was not, as some have often suggested, a torturer of captive sailors nor a mass murderer. But could you convince yourself of that if confronted by one of the supposedly vilest pirates ever to sail the high seas?

The second apparition is sometimes to be found on Gardiner Island. Here, so it is claimed, Captain Kidd returns in order to find his buried treasure. It is a journey that will prove a permanent waste of time. Although carefully hidden, the authorities were fairly thorough in recovering those ill-gotten gains. Lord Bellomont carried out numerous enquiries and eventually recovered the buried cache of hidden wealth that Kidd had hoped to use as a bargaining counter. Although some of it might have disappeared into private hands, the bulk of it was subsequently shipped to London and absorbed into the national coffers.

Another interesting story that concerns a one time pirate

appears in *The Odyssey of an Orchid Hunter* by F. D. Burdett. This also involves buried treasure and a haunted island:

'From the far north of the Philippine Islands . . . we
steered towards the setting sun, with the Babuyan
islands going down in the sea astern; and after
rounding the north-west point of Luzon, swung
due south – through the Mindoro Straits and the
Sulu Sea . . . eventually dropping anchor off the
island of Sarangani.

High on a promontory, towering above the
teeming jungle-growth, two clumps of feathery
palms stand out clearly against the sky. They mark
the grave of Sarangani, the pirate, and the Moros
will tell you that this place is haunted, after nightfall, by the ghosts of his murdered female slaves.
There seems to be something sinister in the hot still
air of this island of ghastly memories. After sun-
down, my pagan crew resolutely refused to set foot
ashore there . . .

With their *vintas*, probably the fastest sailing
ships in the world, they [the Moros] sailed those
turbulent waters. In the good old days – so far as
the Moros are concerned – of piracy, Sarangani,
most notorious buccaneer of them all, plundered,
murdered and raped to his heart's content until his
name was the terror of the Philippines from north
to south. Sarangani was the bloodiest of all the
Moro Datos who made their piratical nests in the
Sulu and Celebes Seas. Even in death the tribes
still fear him . . .

Year after year, Sarangani sailed north on the
south-west monsoon and returned on the north-
east monsoon with cargoes of loot and captive
girls.

Although the Spanish government offered big
rewards for his capture he always gave them the
slip . . .

When his treasure was ready for his secret cache, he ordered it to be embarked on one of his *vintas*, at night by superfluous women slaves who were growing old and unattractive. They were the carriers who bore the treasure to its hiding place. And they never returned to Sarangani Island. Sarangani's deadly treasure boat sailed at night, and he always returned on the following night, alone.

It is not difficult to imagine the terror of the women who were detailed to join these nocturnal expeditions. They knew what it meant . . . They had to assist him bury the treasure . . . and he would bury them with it.

When the old sea-wolf lay dying surrounded by his numerous wives, he only smiled grimly when they asked him to tell them where his treasure was hidden, the gold nest of fifty years of piracy.

He replied, saying, 'Who seeks may find.'

There is no doubt about Sarangani's treasure being buried on the island . . . There must be a number of these buried hecatombs. I know of one place that is absolutely tabu. Legend – or perhaps it is more than that – says that Sarangani himself always warned people that whosoever ventured to visit the unhallowed spot would never be seen again alive.

I have landed on the island and scouted around, but my pagan crew absolutely refused to set foot ashore. There seemed to be some taint in the air, something noisome and sepulchral . . . Something sinister and deadly haunts the sepulchre of murdered slaves and murder's loot.'

This curse of piracy, once the bane of the maritime community, seems to have a natural affinity with the world of ghosts. After all, not only their victims but also many pirates themselves meet with unbelievably violent ends. As a result, so it is often claimed, their spirits are quite incapable of discovering permanent sanctuary. Instead, they are returned to earth for the purpose of haunting the living. Although such folk tales are now invariably dismissed, this ancient belief might well explain why the supposed presence of a pirate ghost ship is to be seen off Galveston, Texas.

As with many such stories, it is difficult to find anyone who has either seen the ship or can describe it in detail. Traditionaly however, it is supposed to be the clipper-built schooner that once belonged to Jean Lafitte. He was another pirate-cum-privateer whose activities were partially concealed by the numerous national wars that marked the first two decades of the 19th century. Sometimes claiming to possess letters of marque from the United States government and at other times stating himself to be in alliance with either Spain or Mexico, Lafitte slowly increased his haul of treasure at the expense of merchantmen who entered the Gulf of Mexico.

During the years leading up to and including the War of 1812 Lafitte's centre of activity was based on the island of Barantaria, just to the south of New Orleans. However, he had become such a thorn in the side of the American authorities that, even given the threat of an impending British invasion of New Orleans, it was decided to remove him from Barantaria. Using a naval force under the command of Commodore Patterson, the island was successfully taken, although Lafitte himself managed to escape. As a result of support that Lafitte gave to the defenders of New Orleans during the subsequent invasion, he was eventually given a full pardon for his earlier illicit activities. Despite this, Lafitte was not yet ready to discard his old ways and decided to set up a new pirate community on the island of Galveston, but this had only a moderate degree of success and Lafitte eventually left the island in his schooner.

It is in this final departure that the stories of Lafitte's continued spiritual presence in the area are firmly rooted. For many years it was believed that Lafitte died shortly after-

The pirate Jean Lafitte. It is said that his spectral ship may occasionally be seen off the Texas coast near Galveston. (Courtesy Rosenberg Library, Galveston, Texas)

wards, with southern Mexico his most frequently declared resting place. However, more recent evidence, albeit contested, suggests this to be incorrect. Apparently, Lafitte did not meet an early fate, but survived for a good many years. In fact, after changing his name, he became a successful businessman operating within the terms of the law.

Given Jean Lafitte's later activities, it seems unlikely that his restless spirit would have returned to the island of Galveston. More likely, the story of the continuing presence of his pirate ship arose from that initial belief in his early demise. As he did not die until 1854 it seems unlikely that he could have been on board a phantom ship whose appearance had, by that date, firmly implanted itself within local folk tradition.

The *Spray* following her successful return to the USA. Did Joshua Slocum really encounter one of Columbus's contemporaries?

3

The Pilot Of The *Pinta*

It is Joshua Slocum who can justly claim the strangest of all encounters with a phantom of the high seas. While on the first leg of his single-handed circumnavigation of the globe the life of this famous American seaman was saved by the timely appearance of a 16th century Spanish navigator!

With incredible determination Slocum started his dramatic lone voyage on April 24th 1895. Giving little thought to the hazards ahead, he had decided on a leisurely voyage that would ultimately keep him away from his home port of Boston for the next three years. At his command was a tiny 36 ft 9 ins vessel that drew just four feet of water. Not inappropriately he named her *Spray*, and in her became the first man to sail round the world single handed.

The *Spray* had begun life a good many years earlier as an oysterman plying the coasts of Delaware. By the time that Slocum had been introduced to this rather minute vessel she had already served a number of different owners. At one time she gave the appearance of being fit for nothing better than the breaker's yard. Indeed, during the seven years which preceded Slocum's purchase of the future *Spray*, she had lain abandoned on a Fairhaven beach, a canvas sheet her only protection from the elements. Yet Slocum had been keen to get hold of just such a vessel. Having found her, he decided upon completely rebuilding her. Settling down to a mammoth task of which he later wrote 'something tangible appeared every day to show for my labour', while 'the neighbours made the work sociable'.

The setting up of the new stem and its fastening to the keel proved a particularly memorable event. According to Slocum:

> 'whaling captains came from far to survey it. With one voice they pronounced it "A1", and in their opinion "fit to smash ice". The oldest captain shook my hand warmly when the breast hooks were put in, declaring that he could see no reason why *Spray* should not "cut in bow-head" yet off the coast of Greenland'.

Not many readers will be familiar with these old whaling terms. 'Cut in bow head' refers to 'flensing' or cutting the blubber from a whale (of the bow head species) into spiral strips.

The actual task of rebuilding *Spray* must have taken a number of years. Slocum is not very clear on this matter, but certainly mentions the passing of several seasons. Throughout this time, the 50 year old Nova Scotia born seaman who had previously commanded square riggers could be found in the task of bending, shaping, hammering, sawing and caulking the various timbers that went into the complete renewal of his beloved *Spray*. Slowly her entire being changed, 'so gradually that it was hard to say at what point the old died or the new took birth'.

Having left American waters on April 24th 1895 Slocum reached the Azores on July 20th. Entering the port of Horta, on the island of Fayal, he chose to relax for a total of four days. Taking his leave on the 24th, he carried on board a strange mixture of food stuffs that included an over plentiful supply of plums and white cheese from the neighbouring island of Pico. Without thought to the effects on his stomach Slocum chose to make these two products the main item of his first evening meal. The outcome was catastrophic.

With heavy seas to the south-west and heightening Atlantic waves, Slocum found himself totally incapacitated. Acute stomach pains and a constant feeling of nausea ended in a long period of unconsciousness. All Slocum had been able to do for the sake of his own safety was to shorten the mainsail and hope for a miracle. As he lay in his bunk, totally oblivious to the world around him, the weather continued to deteriorate. Those earlier efforts at reefing were completely ineffective as the wind steadily mounted. With the *Spray* forging ahead under a dangerous spread of sail, the master was urgently required to further reduce sail area by taking in the jib. But Slocum was in no fit state to undertake this essential task.

It was at this point that the unbelievable took place. With the tiny vessel increasingly battered by the elements, her incapacitated and sole crew member was joined by the ghost of an earlier mariner.

In appearance he was much like the story book pirate, clothed in a leather jerkin, tight leggings and calf length boots. Partially obscuring his weather-beaten face was a shaggy black beard and a large red cap that jauntily covered his left ear. Despite this flamboyant taste in clothes, the intruder was every inch a sailor. Quickly grappling with the wheel, his experienced hands soon returned the *Spray* to a semblance of controlled progress.

Eventually, Slocum regained consciousness. With undoubted surprise, he focussed his eyes on the volunteer helmsman. Somewhat frightened by the situation, he thought the intruder might be there to do him harm. This, the newcomer seemed to realise.

'Senor, I have come to do you no harm,' he declared. 'I have sailed free but was never worse than a smuggler of contraband.'

Slocum gazed at his visitor. Accepting the strange clothes as the rig of a foreign seaman, a series of questions flooded into his mind. Again, the intruder answered the first of these unasked questions.

'I am one of Columbus's crew. I am the pilot of the *Pinta*

The strange apparition that appeared to Joshua Slocum during his single-handed circumnavigation of the globe. Slocum claims that this strangely dressed sailor was responsible for saving his yacht during a night of heavy seas.

come to aid you. Lie quiet señor captain and I will guide your ship tonight.'

Despite having such impeccable credentials, for the *Pinta* was one of the three ships with Columbus on his historic voyage and had been therefore one of the first vessels to make a double crossing of the Atlantic, Slocum still had his doubts. For one thing, the *Spray* still felt as if she was carrying too much sail. Once more the ancient seaman knew what was on Slocum's mind.

'Yonder is the *Pinta* ahead. We must overtake her', he explained. 'Give her sail! Give her sail! Vale, vale, muy vale'

Then the intruder turned his attention to Slocum's sickness. Pushing a quid of black twist into his mouth, he casually informed the amazed Americano that he was wrong to have mixed cheese and plums.

'White cheese is never safe unless you know whence it comes. Quien sabe, it may have been from leche de Capra and becoming capricious . . .'

For the rest of the night, so it would appear, Slocum's new found crew member remained at the wheel. Keeping the *Spray* on her correct and true course, the man from the past was clearly enjoying the experience of sailing the small sloop. At daybreak, with Slocum now slightly recovered, Columbus's borrowed pilot chose to make his return to the *Pinta*. Leastways, when Slocum finally clambered up the companionway steps he found the deck deserted.

The night's storm had certainly taken its toll. As Slocum looked along the length of the *Spray* he saw that the breaking waves had swept her decks clean of all movable objects. In the words he later used in his account of the voyage, the deck was 'now as white as a shark's tooth'. But, despite this battering, the *Spray* had successfully survived the storm. Her sails were intact and she had not been swamped. Even more surprising, the log showed that she had made good 90 miles on her true course.

'Columbus himself,' remarked the amazed Slocum, 'could not have held her more exactly on course.'

It seems most unfortunate that Joshua Slocum was not to be rescued by a return of this welcome intruder some 14 years later. In 1909, and once again sailing the *Spray*, Slocum set off from Bristol, Rhode Island, for the Orinoco. On this occasion he failed to reach port, the lone yachtsman and his craft never to be seen again. Of course, such a journey failed to take him anywhere near the Azores. But the waters he crossed would not have been totally unknown to Columbus and his able pilot. It is possible however, that the perils confronting Slocum were, for some reason, not communicated to his former sailing partner. On the other hand, that final danger may simply have been too great for even a seaman of 400 years standing.

Since Joshua Slocum's disappearance, several suggestions have been put forward as to the fate of this redoubtable lone yachtsman. One theory is that the *Spray* may have been run down at night by a rapidly voyaging steamer. Such vessels are an obvious danger to those operating small craft, while the knowledge available to a 15th century pilot would have been singularly inadequate for the handling of such a situation!

4

The Ghost Of The *Great Eastern*

Shortly after midday the massive *Great Eastern* steamship was launched into the murky and decidedly uninviting waters of London's River Thames. It was an event that many had thought might never occur. Since the first attempted launch four months earlier, a great deal of money and effort had been spent upon getting the *Great Eastern* afloat.

With the rise and fall of each successive spring tide she had remained obstinately stuck. Throughout that period, this would-be colossus of the high seas had taken on the appearance of a floundering beached whale rather than a sleek passenger liner that would one day race across the Atlantic.

The launch, successfully performed on January 31st 1858, allowed the *Great Eastern* to vacate the stinking mud embankments that seemed so unwilling to set her free. Taking up moorings on the Deptford side of the river, she was ready for fitting out. Over the next few months a mass of engine and boiler components were brought on board and steadily assembled within the depths of her huge vacuous hull. Once everything was in place these items of machinery would be responsible for powering her single underwater screw and two paddle wheels. As a further extension of this clear belt and braces principle, the *Great Eastern* was also to witness the stepping of six spindly masts and the arrival of sufficient canvas to cover an entire football pitch.

On each working day, throughout the months of fitting out, a veritable army of engineers, ironsmiths and riggers could be seen clambering around her various decks. Joining them were the carpenters, furnishers and fitters who were building accommodation for 300 passengers.

Each of the cabins was completed to first class standards, the owners of the ship having rejected the idea of transporting those who could only afford steerage or second class accommodation. To ensure that each passenger had full value for money the cabins not only contained a wash basin and fitted dressing table but also a splendid settee designed to hide a bath of generous proportions. This latter feature was a rarity for ships of the period. Even more of a novelty were the taps which gave the bather a choice of fresh hot water or medicinally recommended cold sea water.

Despite the advanced nature of these cabins, they seemed quite mundane when compared with the grand saloon. Stretching a full 62 ft (18.9m) it had a width of 36 ft (11m) and was finished in white, decorously set off with ornamental iron work. It had been designed to be superior to any other saloon on land or sea. Two sets of huge, centrally positioned mirrors not only made a striking feature but effectively concealed two of the ship's funnels that passed straight through the passenger decks at this point.

It was not until September 1859 that the vessel was ready for her first seagoing voyage. Leaving the Thames estuary on the 9th, it was planned that she would sail to Weymouth where, if everything was in order, the owners of the vessel would officially accept her as completed. From Weymouth it was then intended that she should proceed to Holyhead where she would take on passengers for New York.

A particular feature of the *Great Eastern* was the existence of an iron jacket fitted to the base of each funnel. These held water that might be used to feed the boilers, but their main purpose was to prevent the heat emitted from the funnels becoming a fire hazard. However, so hot did the funnels become that the water inside the jackets quickly reached boiling point, making it necessary for the addition of a device through which steam could be released. To undertake this task, each jacket was fitted with a stand pipe that terminated at the top of the funnel. Without these stand pipes the jackets fitted to each of the funnels would have been a greater hazard than the outbreak of fire they were supposed to prevent.

Prior to the *Great Eastern* sailing out of the Thames it had been necessary to test these water jackets up to a pressure of 55 lbs. This had been achieved through the insertion of a stop cock to each of the stand pipes. Once the water inside the jackets had been heated and the pressure measured, the stop cocks had been rapidly opened. Later, it was ordered that the stop cocks should be removed, but it was a task that was only partially completed. For reasons that have never been explained, the stop cocks belonging to the two funnels passing through the grand saloon were never dismantled. Of course, this was not a problem – providing the two remaining stop cocks were never closed.

On board the *Great Eastern* as she left the Thames on that September day in 1858 were a number of engineers responsible for observing how the two sets of engines performed. One of their number, Duncan McFarlane, who was in charge of the paddle engine auxilliaries, made a point of noting that a thin trail of steam was coming from the two forward stand pipes. This was a clear indication that the stop cocks were still open and that there was no likelihood of a dangerous build up of pressure. However, as the *Great Eastern* passed through the Straits of Dover and made a series of essential course alterations for the passage down the English Channel to Weymouth, something inexplicable occurred. The handles of the two stop cocks, safely concealed inside their wooden casings just above the deck level, were forced into the closed position. From that moment onwards, the two iron jackets had been converted from a useful safety feature into an uncontrollable time bomb.

Although the ship itself might well survive the resulting explosion, any passengers in the grand saloon would most certainly be killed. If they managed to escape being smashed

A general view of the *Great Eastern*. Many of her passengers and crew claim to have heard strange noises emanating from the very depths of her hull.

Brunel's *Great Eastern* seen here under construction. Her unique double bottom and transverse bulkheads are clearly to be seen. Within these, it is traditionally believed, a missing riveter was permanently entombed.

into pulp by the huge chunks of iron casing that would be thrown out in all directions they would still have to face the dangers presented by eight tons of boiling water and scalding steam. Nor was this all. Ten thousand slivers of broken glass exploding from the giant ornate mirrors that surrounded these two funnels and their iron jackets would be just as lethal.

The afternoon witnessed a steady increase in the numbers entering the saloon. Apart from senior company staff, they included reporters and a number of fare paying passengers who wished to savour the maiden voyage of this truly unique ship. Between four and six o'clock many of these individuals were drawn to the saloon for the purpose of taking tea or downing a few glasses of Scotch. Little did they realise the danger they were in!

Some of their number may have begun to perspire as a result of increasing heat created by the superheated steam trapped within the two separate 'time bombs'. Nobody thought to ask why the saloon had become so hot.

As the *Great Eastern* drew level with Dungeness, one of those on board had the fortunate idea of going out on deck and taking a look at the historic coastal town of Hastings. After all, it was September, the very month in which William the Conqueror had entered the same stretch of water prior to his famous battle in 1066. Others followed his example and the saloon slowly emptied. Virtually everyone on board seems to have decided that the view might be worth the effort of climbing to the upper deck. A massacre of the innocents had been narrowly avoided.

At around 6pm the inevitable occurred. With a deafening boom, the forward water jacket exploded. Iron, glass, steam and boiling water swept across the full length of the saloon. Only one person, the captain's young daughter, had remained in this area. Miraculously she survived. At the time of the explosion she had been on the far side of a solid wrought iron bulkhead. Anywhere else in the saloon and she would have been literally cut to pieces.

Amongst those on board the *Great Eastern* at the time of the explosion was a reporter from *The Times* of London. He supplied this vivid eyewitness account:

> The forward part of the deck appeared to spring like a mine, blowing the funnel up into the air. There was a confused roar amid which came the awful crash of timber and iron mingled together in frightful uproar and then all was hidden in a rush of steam. Blinded and almost stunned by the overwhelming concussion, those on the bridge stood motionless in the white vapour till they were reminded of the necessity of seeking shelter by the shower of wreck – glass, gilt work, saloon ornaments and pieces of wood which began to fall like rain in all directions.

Although all the passengers and various officials who belonged to the companies that had built and fitted out the *Great Eastern* all survived, there were six fatalities among the crew. These were all firemen who had been working beneath the jacket when it exploded. All of them died in intense agony, suffering one of the most terrible deaths imaginable: they were boiled alive.

However, this could not be the end of the matter. With one jacket giving way to the immense pressure that had built up, the second jacket was also on the verge of exploding. Fortunately, one of the numerous engineers on board was sufficiently alert to the situation, realising that such an explosion almost certainly resulted from the water jacket having been sealed. Giving one of the ship's greasers a key, he ordered him immediately to check the stop cock on the second pipe. Discovering it to be shut, he turned it open. From the top of the stand pipe came an ear splitting whistle as a great cloud of steam forced its way out. A second possible tragedy had been narrowly avoided.

The mysterious shutting of the two stop cocks has, to this day, never been satisfactorily explained. No one has ever come forward and admitted responsibility for this fatal act. But, somehow, the handles of the two closing cocks must have been turned, so creating that dangerous time bomb effect.

Accident or not, this was only one of the many tragedies that eventually struck the *Great Eastern*. Over the next 30 years she was to gain an unenviable reputation. Many, in fact, came to believe that she was a jinxed ship destined to bring unhappiness to those who came into contact with her. And jinxed she may well have been . . .

Apart from the problem of her launch and trial voyage the huge vessel was also a victim of many more accidents. Frequently these involved loss of life. In fact the *Great Eastern* eventually claimed the lives of well over 30 of her crew. Some were mown down by pieces of machinery that became detached without warning, while others drowned when they fell overboard. In addition, the *Great Eastern* also sank or destroyed a total of 10 other vessels, with the loss of life again reaching double figures.

Sometimes, indeed, her very presence at a harbour or port would seem to endanger the surrounding area. On such occasions even the elements seemed to protest, with fires often breaking out in close proximity to the ship. In the Thames-side yard where she was built, for instance, three major fires were reported during the time she was under construction. Other fires were reported in New York, Liverpool and Milford during times when the ship was present.

Another facet of the *Greast Eastern*'s ill-luck was her ability to soak up money while offering little in return. Her first victim was John Scott Russell, owner of the prestigious building yard in which she was constructed. Grossly underestimating the costs involved in building such a vessel, his own company went bankrupt. As a result, she could only be completed once the liquidators had taken the firm over. In turn, many of the companies who became associated with her failed to make a profit, with each of them being forced to sell the ship in order to avoid a similar financial disaster as that suffered by Russell.

Because of this catalogue of unmitigated disasters much thought was given to the question of why she should be such an unlucky ship. Some turned to ancient superstitions for an explanation. It was pointed out that she laboured under the notorious burden of an unsuccessful launch. From time immemorial it has been the belief of mariners that if anything went wrong at a ship's launch, it would reflect on the vessel throughout her entire career. With the *Great Eastern* having undergone several attempted launches, it was widely believed that nothing good would come of her.

Much more persistent was the generally held belief that the *Great Eastern* was haunted. The earliest suggestion of her having a phantom on board occurred during the fitting out period on the Thames. Many of those who worked on the vessel at this time are supposed to have complained of hearing strange hammering sounds coming from the bowels of the vessel. Similar noises were said to be heard immediately before the explosion off Hastings. It has even been suggested that there was a connection and that the sounds were a warning of impending disaster. A number of accounts of the *Great Eastern* also go on to state that these noises were also heard two days later. The ship's captain, William Harrison, reputedly complaining to his chief engineer of being 'rudely awakened by constant hammering from below'. That same night the ship's designer, Isambard Kingdom Brunel, having received news of the boiler explosion, died a disappointed man.

Were the hammering sounds connected? Unfortunately, the amount of truth underpinning these various stories is difficult to estimate. Many writers have glibly accepted a number of the more sensational accounts, going on to repeat them without indicating an original source. In turn, others have repeated and embroidered these same stories. As a result, it is virtually impossible to sort out fact from fiction.

The general belief in the *Great Eastern* being haunted sometimes led those who sailed in the vessel to attribute any of the strange shipboard sounds that they could not immediately identify as being caused by the ship's ghost. Usually such suggestions were ignored by the captain and his senior officers, all of them aware that on such a large and advanced vessel there were bound to be a cacophony of unfamiliar sounds.

In the summer of 1862 one of these unidentifiable sounds was treated just a little more seriously than normal. At the time the *Great Eastern* was moored in New York's Flushing Bay, the vessel having completed an uneventful crossing of the Atlantic. However, upon entering the Bay, she had struck an uncharted rock. This created a gash over 80 ft (24.4m) in length and on which immediate repairs had to be undertaken. This, however, was no easy matter, there being no dry dock large enough to contain the *Great Eastern* on the American side of the Atlantic. Instead, a special cylindrical caisson, large enough to accommodate a gang of riveters, was designed to be fitted over the gash. Held secure by a series of chains, access to the caisson was through a tube which projected above the water.

At first repair work upon the underside of the ship's hull progressed satisfactorily. Then, all of a sudden, the riveters went on strike because during periods in which they were not working, strange hammering sounds had been clearly heard within the dark and cramped space of the caisson. Refusing to re-enter, the riveters seemed convinced it was the ship's ghost warning them of some future disaster.

In order to encourage the riveters to return to their work a thorough search of the *Great Eastern* was immediately undertaken. The newly appointed captain, Walter Evans, decided to check the outside of the ship. Taking a small rowing boat he eventually discovered the cause of the eerie sound that had so disturbed a gang of otherwise hardened riveters. It was nothing more than a heavy swivel hitting the ship's side as it rose and fell with the swell.

Despite events in Flushing Bay during the summer of 1862 the possibility of the *Great Eastern* having a ghost continued to excite the attention of many who boarded the vessel. In particular, interest was frequently directed to the origins of the ghost. Passengers could frequently be heard discussing a number of bizarre and ludicrous stories. Often they would outbid each other in their efforts to entertain fellow passengers with their presumed knowledge.

The flavour of some of these stories can be found in a book entitled *A Floating City*. Written by the science fiction novelist Jules Verne it is a semi-fictional account of a voyage that the author made on board the massive steam ship. Having joined the *Great Eastern* in March 1868, Verne appears to have been barraged with a number of differing stories. One conversationalist knowingly informed him that the ghost was that of a former passenger. Apparently this luckless individual had lost his way in the hold of the ship and had never come out alive! Later, Verne was confidently informed that the ghost belonged to an engineer mistakenly boiled alive in the steam box.

Although not mentioned by Jules Verne, there is one explanation for the supposed haunting of the ship which has proved remarkably durable. This is the suggestion that the ghost was a former member of a riveting gang entombed in the vessel while she was under construction. More precisely, it is usually held that the trapped man was a basher, one of those responsible for hammering the rivet once it had been carefully positioned by another member of the work gang. In stating this to be the case, those who claim that the ghost is a former basher indicate as evidence the design of the ship. The *Great Eastern* was the first ship to be designed with a double bottom. The construction was almost as if there were two hulls built one inside the other and separated by a series of longitudinal and transverse bulkheads. It was this particular design feature that saved the *Great Eastern* from sinking when she struck the uncharted rock at the entrance to Flushing Bay, and double bottoms soon became standard shipbuilding practice.

It was within one of these compartments of the double bottom that it is supposed the basher was trapped. A possible scenario is that the man (and in some versions he is joined by a boy assistant) was somehow rendered unconscious shortly before the compartment was sealed. Once revived, the injured basher found himself in a low ceilinged room that had no form of communication with the outside world. His immediate reaction was to maintain a relentless hammering upon the iron bulkheads that surrounded him. However hard he banged, his desperate pleas went unanswered, the sound of his hammering merging into the general background noise created by the other 200 bashers employed on the ship. The hammering heard so long after the basher (and the young lad with him) had died, was considered to be the man's spirit attempting its escape from this same unwelcome resting place.

The final breaking up of the *Great Eastern*, was carried out in the late 1880s by the Birkenhead firm of Henry Bath and Company. It was a task accompanied by a degree of morbid interest. Many felt that the skeletal remains of the basher and his lad would eventually be found.

According to at least one account of the famous ship, the believers in this particular story were not disappointed. In his book *The Great Iron Ship* the author, James Dugan, includes part of a letter that was sent to him by David Duff, a tug captain in Birkenhead when the *Great Eastern* was broken up. According to Duff, a gang of breakers working on the ship 'found a skeleton inside the ship's shell and the tank tops'.

At last, therefore, some hard physical evidence . . . or was it? David Duff, for his part, did not state that he saw the skeleton or who found it. Apart from blandly declaring it to be 'the skeleton of the basher who was missing' he had very little to add. In fact, he was almost certainly repeating a rumour that was probably going the rounds of Liverpool and Birkenhead at the time. With so many people expecting a skeleton to be found, it hardly seems surprising that a rumour to this effect was eventually started. After all, teams of ship breakers have to have something to break the monotony or excite their humour!

If such a skeleton had been found then documentary evidence would also exist. However, neither the company records of Henry Bath and Sons, the local coroners' court nor any newspaper reveal anything further about the dramatic find. In other words, there was no find! David Duff, like so many before and after, was taken in by the rumour of the missing riveter.

Moving back to some of the other points in the story these, too, lack credibility when placed under the microscope. First and foremost is the matter of whether a basher went missing during construction of the ship. Although this is a frequently cited 'fact', there is no evidence. Several riveters certainly died while on board the ship, but none actually went missing. Possibly it was the death of one of these bashers that might have started the story in the first place.

Furthermore, there is the matter of these tiny watertight compartments in which the 'missing basher' became trapped. As it happens, they were not sealed at the time of the *Great Eastern*'s construction, and inspection holes remained open for at least a year. It was only after several crossings of the Atlantic that they were finally closed.

Overall, it must be concluded that Brunel's mighty ship was not haunted by the ghost of a trapped riveter. There is too much evidence to the contrary. As to whether the ship was haunted by some other ghost, there is always the matter of the long lost passenger . . .

Repair work begins on the *Great Eastern* following the horrendous explosion off Hastings during September 1859. It is traditionally believed that the phantom she carried on board tried to give warning of the impending disaster.

The *Great Eastern* was packed with a mass of complex machinery. Although many would deny it, others would suggest that this was the real cause of the unidentified tapping noises said to be caused by the ghost of the entombed riveter.

5

The Transparent Lady
A True Ghost Story?

One of the most fascinating accounts of a haunted ship appeared in a turn of the century edition of the *Pembroke County Guardian*. It was written by Commander George Manley Alldridge and concerned HMS *Asp*, a small paddle steamer that he once commanded.

Alldridge was appointed to the vessel during the early part of 1850 and joined her while she was undergoing her annual refit at Portsmouth dockyard. The commander was certainly no believer in ghosts and was highly sceptical of numerous reports that told of *Asp* having been haunted for a number of years. Amongst those who approached him on the subject was the dockyard's Admiral-Superintendent.

'Do you know sir, your ship is said to be haunted?' was the rather unusual remark with which the admiral introduced himself. 'I don't know if you will get any of the dockyard men to work on her,' the admiral continued.

'I don't care for ghosts,' Alldridge respectfully replied. 'I dare say I shall get her all to right fast enough.'

At first the dockyard shipwrights working on the re-fit continued to perform their numerous tasks without complaint. After about a week however, they showed themselves to be less than happy with the vessel. Approaching Alldridge, they too claimed the vessel to be haunted. Indeed, they even begged him 'to give up the vessel' believing she would bring Alldridge nothing but ill-luck.

Of course, it was highly unlikely that a newly appointed officer would give up his command on the advice of a few dockyard 'mateys'. As for the ghost itself, Alldridge had seen neither hide nor hair of this supposed apparition and had no reason to fear its presence. He was also aware that the dockyard 'mateys' of Portsmouth were more than capable of invention. In the past a number of carefully contrived jokes had led to the reddened faces of many a junior officer. Alldridge was not going to be one such victim!

Despite the oft repeated fears of those who worked on the vessel the task of repairing some minor faults to her machinery and the re-coppering of her hull was finally completed. Hauling away from the harbour quayside on May 26th 1850 HMS *Asp* made an uneventful voyage to North Wales. Her destination was the River Dee as Commander Alldridge had been ordered to undertake an extensive survey of the estuary. It was while moored in these waters that Alldridge himself first became aware of *Asp*'s additional crew member.

During the evenings it had become customary for Alldridge to invite the ship's master (or as we should now say, Navigating Officer), to his cabin, the two of them spending a few pleasant hours reading to each other. On such occasions, so Alldridge later confided to readers of the *Pembroke County Guardian*, they were 'frequently interrupted by strange noises, often such as would be caused by a drunken man or staggering about which appeared to issue from the after cabin'.

This after cabin was only a few feet away from where the two of them spent their time reading, the two cabins separated by only a narrow passageway that gave access to the companion ladder. On the first occasion upon which they heard this noise it was so loud that they assumed furniture was being moved by the steward.

'Don't make such a noise,' cried out George MacFarlane, the master. With this, the noise temporarily ceased, only to begin again after a few minutes. This time the sound of moving furniture was even louder.

'What are you doing, steward?' called out MacFarlane. By

now, the master was decidedly angry. 'Why are you making such a bloody noise?' Receiving no reply he grabbed the candle and bounded across the passageway to the after cabin, but was surprised to discover the compartment completely empty. Returning to Alldridge's cabin, the two of them decided to put the matter to one side and resumed their reading. As they did so the silence was again shattered by a further outburst of noise that appeared to be coming from the same cabin.

Alldridge was by now more than a little concerned. He decided to take a look for himself. This time, so he felt, a careful search of the cabin would soon reveal a drunken crew member either hidden in one of the cupboards or taking refuge behind the bunk. But after checking out every nook and cranny he too, was amazed to find nothing.

Over the following months, according to Alldridge's own account, 'the noise became very frequent, varying in kind and degree. Sometimes it was as though the seats and lockers were being banged about, sometimes as though decanters and tumblers were being clashed together. During these disturbances the vessel was lying more than a mile off shore.'

In particular Alldridge remembered when he and Mac-Farlane were both invited to take tea at a friend's house in Queensferry. At the time *Asp* was moored alongside opposite Church's Quay. Returning at about 10pm, Alldridge was descending the companionway when he clearly heard someone rush from the after cabin into the fore cabin. Both he and MacFarlane were certain someone was down there.

'Stand still!' Alldridge commanded his fellow officer. 'I think I have caught the ghost!' Passing a sword back up to the master, he gave one further instruction, 'Now allow no one to pass you. If anyone attempts to escape, cut him down. I will stand the consequences.'

With this, Alldridge entered his own cabin, determined to flush out this intruder. Once more, he was to be disappointed. Proceeding to strike a match, he found both this, the after cabin and passageway to be completely devoid of human life. Yet he had been absolutely certain that someone was there. As he again confided to readers of his newspaper article, 'there was nothing to be done, but to report for the hundredth time, "Well, it's the ghost again!"'

Noises associated with this supernatural presence on board *Asp* now became even more frequent. Sometimes it was as if drawers in the after cabin were being opened and closed, while at other times the noises were similar to those made by a bed being pulled around. Often Alldridge would lie awake at night convinced that objects were being moved in his own cabin. A spare bunk opposite his own would sometimes take on a life of its own, while at other times there might be a heavy thump that sounded like the wash stand being thrown to the floor. Even more worrying however, was the sound of an exploding gun!

The first glimpse that anyone appears to have had of this elusive Spectre was when *Asp* was at anchor one evening in Martyn Roads. It was then that a lookout reported seeing the figure of a young lady standing on the paddle box, her fingers pointing towards heaven. Although Alldridge chose to dismiss this first sighting, it appears that this same young lady was seen on many further occasions.

Another who came into contact with the ghost was the officers' steward. This was on a Sunday afternoon when *Asp* was lying in the Haverfordwest River, opposite Lawrenny. All other members of the crew, including Alldridge, were ashore. As the steward descended the companion ladder he was spoken to by someone standing nearby. Yet, despite it being daylight, he was quite unable to see the owner of the voice. It was an incident that very much shocked the steward and the man subsequently asked the commander for his discharge.

According to Alldridge the *Asp* lost a good number of men during the years in which he commanded the vessel. His newspaper account states that some 'even ran away on being refused their discharge, and a great many others I felt forced to let go, so great was their fear, one and all telling me the same tale, namely, that at night they saw the transparent figure of a lady pointing with her finger up to heaven. For many years I attempted to ridicule the affair, as I was often put to considerable inconvenience by the loss of hands, but to no purpose'.

It was during the year 1857 that the ghost made a sudden and unheralded departure. In November of that year *Asp* was taken into the dockyard at Pembroke for re-coppering and general repairs. On the first night, while tied up to the dock-yard wall, one of the guards patrolling the yard saw a woman, her hand pointing towards the sky, mount the paddle box and then step ashore.

'Who goes there?' he queried.

Although armed with a musket, the guard felt no sense of security. Failing to receive any form of answer from the woman the guard simply dropped his musket and ran for all he was worth. A second sentry, who saw all this take place, fired off his own musket, with the intention of warning the rest of the guard. In the meantime, the apparition managed to glide past a third guard before entering the ruins of Old Pater church. This final guard, in shocked disbelief, stood mesmer-ised as he watched the figure clamber on to one of the graves in the churchyard. Standing still for a moment, with a finger still pointing into the air, the guard saw her slowly disappear.

Concluding the story in Alldridge's own words, 'the ser-geant of the guard came, with rank and file, to learn the tale, and the fright of the sentries all along the dockyard wall was so great that none would remain at their post unless they were doubled, which they were, as may be seen by the Report of the Guard for that night. Singularly enough, since that, the ghost has never been heard of again on board *Asp*, and I never heard the noises which before had so incessantly an-noyed me'.

Would it be possible to find any verification of this strange story? After all it is not impossible that the entire account was nothing more than a tale designed to entertain readers of the *Pembroke County Guardian*. The paddle steamer *Asp* might well never have existed, while the name Alldridge could well have been chosen as a nom-de-plume. So I set out to check these facts from other sources.

The easiest thing to check was the vessel herself. According to Alldridge she was used by the navy for surveying the rivers and seaways around the coast of Wales, but had been used as a mail packet running the route between Portpatrick in Scotland and the Irish port of Donaghadee before being acquired by the Royal Navy.

The easiest way of checking her naval credentials was by reference to one of the many books that list all ships known to have entered the Royal Navy. Amongst these, Jim Colledge's *Ships of the Navy: An Historical Index* is the most outstanding. A quick glance through the pages of this book soon reveals that *Asp* was, indeed, a naval paddle steamer. According to the two line entry that appears in this book, the vessel formerly belonged to the General Post Office and had then carried the name *Fury*.

So the vessel certainly existed but what of her commander? A further book, this time the *Biographical Dictionary of Living Naval Officers* published in 1847, revealed that Alldridge was, indeed, a commissioned officer in the Royal Navy. His full name is given as George Manley Alldridge and he entered the service as a second class volunteer in July 1829. Working his way up through the ranks, he was promoted to lieutenant in February 1844 while serving on board *Firefly*.

Turning more specifically to events mentioned in the *Pembroke County Guardian* I next made a visit to the Public Record Office situated near Kew Gardens in London. Here, within the massive vaults of this recently completed building is housed a mass of material relating to the nation's history, including all of the surviving log books and journals of ships that have served in the Royal Navy. A search through a number of index volumes shows that among log books to have survived from the 19th century are a whole series for the survey vessel *Asp*.

To a certain extent these proved just a little disappointing. While they did confirm that Alldridge had once been her commander and that she had sailed into the River Dee during this period, the log books gave no hint of a possible ghost. Instead of entries such as 'entire crew disturbed by strange noises' I could only find the more innocuous 'crew employed in pumping out bilges' and in place of 'transparent female seen on paddle box' there was only 'employed cleaning engines' or 'crew away in boats surveying'!

Although a number of other documents relating to *Asp* are to be found in the Public Record Office, there appear to be no plans relating to her design. This was also unfortunate. Some sort of drawing would, at least, confirm the existence of the two cabins divided by only a narrow passage leading to the companionway ladder. However, I did think it was possible that the Post Office Archives in South East London might come to the rescue, since the vessel had originally been built as a mail carrying packet for the General Post Office.

Although I was disappointed to discover that no plans existed there either, my visit to the Post Office archives did elicit some further details about the earlier history of the *Asp*. She had been built at Harwich in 1823 and engined on the River Thames by Boulton and Watt. She was first placed on the Dover to Ostend mail run, then transferred to Portpatrick in Scotland in 1831.

This last piece of information reminded me of something else – something I have so far neglected to mention. Commander Alldridge, in that original article, had gone on to indicate that he had tried to account for his vessel being haunted. In doing so, he had also discovered the Portpatrick connection. For a moment therefore, it is worth returning to the actual words used by Alldridge: 'Some years ago, previous to my having her, the *Asp* had been engaged in the mail packet between Portpatrick and Donaghadee. After one of her trips, the passengers having all disembarked, the stewardess, on going into the ladies' cabin, found a beautiful girl with her throat cut, lying in one of the sleeping berths, quite dead. How she came by her death no one could tell me, and though, of course, strict investigations were commenced, neither who she was or where she came from, or anything about her, was ever discovered. The circumstances gave rise to much talk, and the vessel was remanded by the authorities, and she was not again used until handed over to me for surveying service'.

At the time I had hoped that the Post Office archives might have contained something on this incident. However, my hopes were dashed on this point. Besides which *Asp*, although she was commissioned into the navy in 1837, was retained as a mail packet on the Portpatrick to Donaghadee crossing for a further 11 years – a period for which there are no log books to be found in the Public Record Office. In 1848 she was taken off the Portpatrick station and transferred to the naval yard at Keyham for extensive repairs that included re-boilering. If, as Alldridge states, the young woman's death resulted in the vessel being 'remanded' and not returned to service until he took over the vessel, then the death must have occurred somewhere around that year of 1848.

It would, of course, be natural to expect such a violent death to be recorded in various national and local newspapers. Armed only with a vague notion as to a possible date, I decided to test out Alldridge's discovery. Using the facilities of the British Newspaper Library in North London I first scanned *The Times* index for the appropriate period. Unfortunately, there appeared to be no entry that seemed to relate to what I was looking for. Similarly, I could find no reference to such a death in the *Galloway Advertiser and Wigtonshire Free Press*', a newspaper which covered the Portpatrick area during that period.

Despite my inability to confirm Allridge's discovery of a

mysterious death on board *Asp* prior to his taking command, I do not believe it invalidates the possibility of such an event. After all, Alldridge probably acquired the information from men who may have served on board the vessel during its time as a mail packet. In this case, their memories may not have been totally accurate as to the date of the death. Maybe the vessel was returned to service sooner than they believed, making the death a few years earlier than those that I checked.

Moving away from the mysterious death, it must be accepted that in all other areas, the information given by Alldridge is completely accurate. As indicated by log books and other reference material, it is clear that Alldridge served on board the vessel during the period stated. Given that he must also be considered an experienced and trusted naval officer, then it must also be accepted that his account of events on board *Asp* are also likely to be correct. In other words, the *Asp* was haunted.

Less easy to prove is the origin of her ghost. Given the lack of a plausible alternative, it is probably the case that Alldridge's discovery of a mysterious death is also correct. In other words, the sounds he frequently heard were somehow connected with the woman in her death throes, with the apparition finally leaving the vessel in order to discover a more fitting place in which to rest in peace. One only hopes that the spirit of the young lady did find such a haven.

6

A Malevolent Ghost?

NEW YORK, Thursday April 25th 1918. With American troops becoming increasingly involved in frantic Allied efforts to stem a series of German advances on the Western Front, casualty lists were an all too frequent addition to the city's various daily newspapers. On that day alone, *The Evening Post*, on sale throughout Greater New York, indicated American troop losses from the current spring offensive to be in the region of 200. In addition, the United States Marine Corps had announced it had sustained 274 casualties since America's entry into the war.

Despite this sacrifice of American blood, many New Yorker's were showing little real interest in the war. Local recruitment into the armed services left much to be desired, while sales of the recent third issue of American War Bonds or Liberty Bonds was surprisingly low. In analysing this situation, *The Herald* accused the city of an unusual bout of 'lethargy' and pleaded with its readers to buy their full share of bonds.

In an attempt to reverse this state of affairs, the more enthusiastic supporters of the war were fully occupied in preparing a massive 'Win-the-War' parade that was scheduled for the following day. Thousands of soldiers, sailors and patriotic workers were due to march along Fifth Avenue, accompanied by massed bands and numerous local dignitaries. Special attention, throughout, was to be placed on 'the cars of honour'. Each contained mothers whose sons had eagerly volunteered to fight. In one of these cars there were

The American liner St Paul armed and camouflaged. In 1918 she was to suffer an extraordinary accident that was highly coincidental in the exactness of its timing. [United States Naval Institute]

two mothers who could each proudly boast that six of their sons were now on their way to the Western Front.

Unequalled in its support of the war was the famous department store of Wannamakers. Over the next five days, so a series of advertisements proudly proclaimed, the store's gross takings would be converted entirely into Liberty Bonds. Furthermore, customers to this store were informed of a number of special afternoon lectures. Among topics to be covered were the present state of the European war and the importance of buying bonds.

For those who could afford it, Wannamaker's had no shortage of goods to purchase. Proving particularly popular, unlike the War Bonds, were a new range of men's shirts selling at 95c. For the younger female the store had also taken recent delivery of dresses in the style of the day. Described as 'white voile smocked in gold and green' these could be bought for $5. Much more in line with the martial spirit of the day, those intending to enlist could purchase regular army lockers for $11.

Because of the war much of New York's industry had been directed to the needs of the military. A number of dockside companies were involved in the repairing of warships or converting passengers ships into troop carriers. The steam ship *St Paul*, for instance, a massive liner and once the pride of the America Line, was now in the hands of the Robins Dry Dock and Repair Company of Brooklyn. They had been ordered to rip out much of her internal furnishings so that more room would be available for the carriage of troops and their equipment.

With work on the *St Paul* completed, she left Brooklyn early that morning, accompanied by a pair of tugs to take her to Pier 61 at the foot of West 21st Street. The ship was cranky and riding high in the water, due to her having little ballast on board, so the task had to be undertaken with considerable care. However, the man in charge of the vessel, Captain A. R. Mills, was an experienced seaman who knew the *St Paul*.

He had commanded her during a number of recent trans-Atlantic voyages.

When the steamer swung her 535 feet broadside to the strong tide that was racing down the Hudson, it was noticed that she had a slight list to port. Initially there was little concern. It was assumed her crew were involved in filling the ballast tanks and any list would soon be corrected. Approaching Pier 61, two hawsers were thrown out from the *St Paul's* bow and stern. These were secured to the south side of the jetty. A few moments later the liner's two steam winches began to wind in the hawsers. As they did so, the vessel took on a further list.

This, in itself, might have been of little consequence had it not been for a sudden and unexpected inrush of water. Hundreds of tons of the murky Hudson River began to pour into the lower decks, causing the vessel's centre of gravity to shift dramatically. Within a few minutes her heavy masts were scraping against the side of the pier, which only served to push the vessel back into the main channel.

Alongside the *St Paul*, and caught by her as she turned, were a number of barges. These were responsible for saving a number of lives as men jumped to safety. They included members of a naval gun crew, part of her regular complement and workmen from the Robins yard. Many had gone over the side on ropes, while others simply slid down the sloping hull.

For several minutes men poured from the interior of the vessel and got away as best they could. The tugs, which had accompanied the *St Paul* into the River Hudson, also assisted in the rescue, while small boats put out from the shore and picked large numbers out of the water. In this way, all but four of a total of 400 on board were saved.

As for the *St Paul*, once she had been forced out into deep water she continued to turn over. Eventually she came to rest on the bottom, starboard side up.

The sudden and unexpected loss of this valuable liner naturally resulted in attention being given to the possibility of sabotage. Rumours abounded. Some suggested that enemy aliens had intended to sink the steamship in the channel while on her way up the Hudson River. This, so it was firmly believed, was to interfere with the movement of shipping entering and leaving the port. Others even thought they knew how it had been achieved. They suggested it had been carried out by specially trained saboteurs dressed as American workmen. On entering the ship, they had loosened several plates below the waterline, so causing the ship to flood. Eventually this, and numerous similar suggestions, were dismissed.

Before salvaging the vessel, divers carefully examined the hull and discovered exactly why there had been a sudden inrush of water. It appears that one of the ports near the waterline, used for disposing of ash from the boilers, had been left open. Despite a thorough investigation, in which every member of the crew was interviewed, no reason was ever discovered for the port being open.

However, there was one possibility that was not considered at the time. It is possible that the *St Paul* was sunk by a malevolent ghost!

The clue is in the date. The American liner *St Paul* turned over and sank exactly ten years after she had crashed into a naval warship while in British waters. In fact, allowing for differences in time zones, the accident to the *St Paul*, while she was in the Hudson, took place not only 10 years later to the day, but at the exact same hour. Is it not possible, therefore, that one of those who drowned as a result of the tragedy may have returned to haunt the American liner? Enraged by the running down of a fine ship, such a phantom may have determined upon the destruction of the *St Paul*, choosing the 10th anniversary as the most appropriate day for seeking this revenge.

Turning the clock back to the morning of April 25th 1908, the *St Paul* was undergoing final preparations for an immediate departure from Southampton. At this time she was still a relatively new ship launched some 13 years earlier from the yard of the Cramp Ship and Engine Building Company of Philadelphia. With machinery that could develop over 20,000 hp, her twin screws were capable of driving the *St Paul* at a maximum speed of 21.5 knots.

To American eyes she was an elegant ship. Supporters of the owning company, the American Line, drew attention to her straight sweeping bow, 'the long, fine Yankee sheer' and plain uncluttered masts. To those who preferred to give their allegiance to the rival Cunard and White Star Lines, the *St Paul* was a rather ugly ship. They found it difficult to accept the seemingly unnecessary height of her funnels (or 'smoke-stacks' as the Americans insisted on calling them) and the massive bulk of a very high sided hull.

This debate even continued into discussion of her internal layout. Compared with most other Atlantic liners, the *St Paul* offered little in the way of lavish decor that had become part and parcel of an Atlantic crossing. Her grand saloon was plain and simple, its only frivolity that of a pipe organ. Massive glass mirrors, gold leaf trimmings and other luxuries had all been abandoned on the *St Paul*.

In part, this was because the vessel had been built with a second purpose in view. Apart from her use as a passenger carrying liner, Congress had also demanded that she might, in wartime, be easily converted into a fast gun-carrying cruiser. On such occasions, any trimmings that she might possess, would be simply ripped out and doubtless lost or damaged in the process.

During the period of the Cuban War this option was actually taken up. The *St Paul*, one moment a commercial passenger liner running peacefully between Southampton, Cherbourg and New York, was only a few weeks later carrying a battery of 6in. guns that were designed to take on the might of the Spanish navy. During that period of militarisation she proved herself a useful addition to the blockading fleet. Not only did she capture the blockade running British collier *Restormel*, but engaged the Spanish destroyer *Terror* and the sloop *Isabel II*, forcing the *Terror* ashore after damaging her steering gear. Another useful achievement of the *St Paul* during those hostilities was the cutting of the Atlantic cable connecting the island of Cuba to mainland Spain.

Shortly after her return to the American Line the *St Paul* achieved something else noteworthy, giving her a firm anchorage in the annals of maritime history. This was in 1899 when she became the first liner to communicate messages by wireless. At the time she had on board Guglielmo Marconi who had indicated that as the vessel approached the Needles receiving station on the Isle of Wight he would broadcast a message. At 4.45pm on November 15th 1899, contact was established:

'Is that you, *St Paul*?'

'Yes.'

'Where are you?'

'66 nautical miles away.'

However, all this has taken us away from Southampton on that April morning in 1908 where the *St Paul* had boarded her passengers and a general cargo of freight. One of the last to walk up the gangway was the Trinity House pilot, George William Bowyer. It was his job to navigate her safely out of the harbour and through the confined waters of the Solent. Once this part of the *St Paul*'s voyage had been completed he would return control of the vessel to her commander, Captain Frederick McClay Passow and depart.

The weather on that particular day left much to be desired. Snow blizzards were forecast, with much of Southern England already covered in low dense cloud which was down to sea level in places. Normally, the last few days of April can be rather pleasant. More often than not the sun will have a certain warmth, chasing out the final vestiges of the long winter it has usually supplanted. On this particular April day winter was having its final fling.

From Southampton Water, the *St Paul* entered the Solent, making a speed of 21 knots as she passed along the north coast of the Isle of Wight. Her intended course would eventually take her through the narrow gap created at the west end of the Solent by a thrusting shingle spit of land known as Hurst Point. Once passed this particular obstacle, the *St Paul* would enter the English Channel. Having temporarily reduced speed, a return to the earlier 21 knots would be allowed, this being maintained until she approached Cherbourg. Here, as on most of her previous voyages, she would pick up the bulk of her passengers, all of them to be carried to New York.

As the *St Paul* approached the narrowing Hurst Channel the Trinity House pilot, George Bowyer, ordered a reduction to half speed. These instructions appeared to coincide with a definite worsening of the weather. Earlier snow flurries were now being whipped, by a force eight gale, into a veritable blizzard. With visibility now less than 800 yards some were later to suggest that an even greater reduction in speed should have been called for. However, Bowyer was also aware of the *St Paul*'s size, calculating that a good turn of speed was essential if she was to maintain steerage.

On the bridge numerous eyes were attempting to pierce the gloom. To begin with not a single ship could be seen nor distant siren heard. Then, as if emerging from a closed curtain, there appeared the outline of another vessel. This was HMS *Gladiator*, a second class protected cruiser of the Royal Navy returning from Portland to her home port of 'Pompey' as Portsmouth is affectionately known to the Navy. She was on a collision course with the liner, only half a mile separating the two vessels.

To begin with those on board the *St Paul* concentrated upon reducing their own closing speed. To this end Bowyer, who had been giving all bridge commands since the departure from Southampton, ordered all engines to be stopped. However, this in itself, would only have a limited effect. With a ship of this size stopping the engines would not reduce her speed in time to prevent a collision which was only moments away. For this reason, having ordered two blasts to be made on the siren to indicate his intentions, Bowyer telegraphed the engine room, 'full speed astern with the starboard engine'.

On board the cruiser Captain Walter Lumsden RN was aware of the large liner emerging from the grey bank of snow that had fallen across the Solent. His speed was a slightly more cautious nine knots. Uncertain of what action the liner might take, he also ordered the engines to be stopped. Following a return blast on his own siren, he instructed the helmsman to make '30 degrees starboard helm', which was perfectly hard-a-starboard. The effect of this move would be to veer his own ship round to port.

Lumsden had, in fact, got a serious problem on his hands. The international regulation procedure for two vessels approaching each other head-on and in danger of collision is to pass portside to portside. For the *Gladiator* this was just not possible. The available area of sea room prevented such a manoeuvre. Lumsden's instructions to put the helm to starboard was an attempt to pass the *St Paul* on the starboard side.

This decision, combined with the *St Paul* going full astern with the starboard engine, proved to be HMS *Gladiator*'s death sentence. As *St Paul*'s bow slewed to the right, the cruiser now began to present her own starboard side to the liner's bow. It effectively reversed the entire situation. Whereas *Gladiator* had initially been on a direct course that would have punched her own bow into the liner, the American ship was now on course to hit *Gladiator*.

Captain Passow made one final effort to reduce speed, ordering both engines to be reversed. It did little to stop the inevitable. At approximately 2.38pm the *St Paul*'s bow drove into the starboard side of HMS *Gladiator*, at a point reckoned to be just aft of the 67th frame, the fore end of the after stoke hold. The American ship by that time was travelling at a speed of about three knots, but even this was sufficient for a

H. M. S. "Gladiator."
July 1899.

HMS Gladiator at Portsmouth. In 1908 she collided with the American liner *St Paul*. As a result of a strange coincidence the *St Paul* herself capsized in the Hudson River exactly ten years later to the very hour.

gigantic liner to inflict considerable damage on the much smaller British warship.

Cut off from the outside world, and totally oblivious to the impending danger, the stokers deep in the bowels of *Gladiator* had little chance of fleeing to safety. As a result, most of those employed in the after part of the vessel were seriously injured as the liner forced her way through the hull and exposed the boiler room to the inrush of sea water. According to one report the boiler itself burst, enveloping part of the vessel in a cloud of steam. This caused further injury, a number of stokers suffering severe burns and scalds.

As the *St Paul* proceeded to back out, many tons of water poured into the interior of *Gladiator*, giving her a tremendous list to starboard. That she did not founder was due to her watertight bulkhead doors having been promptly closed. At the same time, collision mats were placed over the damaged hull. These were large squares of rope and canvas carried by most British warships and, once thrown over the damaged area, would be held tight against the hull by the pressure of seawater. However, as far as *Gladiator* was concerned, the extensive nature of the rent prevented them working effectively.

With her remaining forward boilers working to high pressure to give the engines full steam ahead, the *Gladiator*'s stem was turned to shore. Making a steady speed towards the Isle of Wight, Captain Lumsden managed to steer her out of the deep water channel before the cruiser became unmanageable from the weight of several thousand tons of seawater. As *Gladiator* touched the bottom close inshore she finally lurched over to one side.

About nine minutes elapsed from the time of the collision to the beaching. Some of the men dived off and swam ashore while others clung to bits of wreckage until rescued. Another group, who could not get to the boats, remained standing on the keel. When *Gladiator* turned over this remained above the level of the water and eventually they too were rescued, some of them taken off by lifeboats belonging to the *St Paul*. Thus a disaster of appalling magnitude was averted, for had *Gladiator* gone down in deep water then there would have been few survivors. As it happened, the final death toll was miraculously restricted to 27.

That the *St Paul* was able to offer help through the launch of her own lifeboats was due to her being relatively un-damaged. Admittedly, the stem of the liner was completely broken with crushed plating pushed round to the vessel's starboard side. However, the closing of the watertight doors sealed this area, with only a small amount of water entering the ship.

Having satisfied himself that the *St Paul* was not in a sinking condition Captain Passow gave the orders for lifeboats to offer all possible assistance to the stranded members of *Gladiator*'s crew. This proved a more difficult task than might at first be imagined. It took 20 minutes before the last of five lifeboats entered the water. Crew members trying to lower them being hampered by blasts of icy wind and ropes caked in snow. Once launched these lifeboats did valuable service, making several journeys and rescuing over 100 of the *Gladiator*'s crew. Among those saved was Captain Lumsden who, with other senior officers was brought to the *St Paul* in the last of the returning lifeboats.

Once the rescue work was complete, the damaged liner set course back to Southampton where a full inspection of her hull could be undertaken. On Tuesday April 28th therefore, the liner was placed in the Alexandra graving dock and, after the water was pumped out, the degree of damage was found to be greater than at first realised. Apart from her broken stem, she was found to have a large gaping cavity that ex-tended inwards for about 20 ft. Within this area was found a large piece of *Gladiator*'s armour plating which had been driven in like a wedge. Indeed, the end was curled upwards about three or four feet inside the liner. A section of a bulkhead and watertight door, also belonging to *Gladiator* was also firmly fixed in the hole.

St Paul had to remain in dry dock for several weeks. The America Line was determined to get her back to sea as soon as possible, sanctioning payments sufficient to ensure that work on the damaged hull could continue round the clock. In the meantime, Captain Lumsden faced an Admiralty court martial. Here the matter of the liner's speed was critically examined, but eventually members of the court concluded that Captain Lumsden was also partly to blame. In particular, they felt that he should still have endeavoured to pass the American liner to port, those sitting in judgement not being entirely convinced that *Gladiator* would automatically have grounded. Lumsden was found guilty of hazarding his ship and sentenced to a severe reprimand.

Having now recounted this earlier incident relating to the *St Paul* it is interesting to speculate on that incredible co-incidence in both date and time. Is it possible that one of those who were drowned in this tragedy took a supernatural exception to the *St Paul*'s speed? Noting that those on board the *St Paul*, had not been exonerated, but had nevertheless escaped punishment, was it possible that this same spirit had decided to take direct action?

How else did that ash port get opened on April 25th 1918? Was it possible that it was an unseen and invisible hand? As already mentioned, the American authorities themselves never came up with an explanation. If a supernatural world of ghosts and phantoms does exist, then perhaps some of their number feel forced to mete out their own justice!

Unlike the *Gladiator*, which was sold for scrap once she had been raised, the *St Paul* did survive beyond that mysterious accident which took place in the Hudson River. Following her refloating in November 1918, she was returned to dry dock for repair. With the war now over, and the world short of valuable passenger liners, it was decided that she should be refurbished. Eventually, at a cost of $1m, the *St Paul* was returned to her former glory, able to embark upon a new, if short-lived, Atlantic career. Unfortunately, the poor state of her engines proved to be her downfall on this occasion and the *St Paul* was finally scrapped in the old Imperial naval dockyard of Wilhelmshaven in 1923.

Opposite:
The cruiser *Gladiator* following her refloating. Seen here in dry dock, the fatal gash caused by the American liner can be seen on the vessel's port bow. Providence, or a malevolent ghost, revenged itself upon the *St Paul*.

HMS GLADIATOR IN DRY DOCK

7

Phantom Ships

Ghosts seem to take many strange and unusual forms, but there can be nothing more puzzling than an entire ship returning to the same waters in which she was once destroyed. Yet, on numerous occasions, various hard headed seamen claim to have seen the apparition of vessels that have long since ended their days on the sea bed.

One reported sighting of a supposed maritime spectre was of a former 6,000 ton Norwegian freighter that carried the name *Tricolor*. Owned by a certain Wilhelm Wilhelmsen, a small time entrepreneur who managed a number of similar ships, the *Tricolor* spent most of her sea going days plying the lucrative trade route that stretched between Europe and the Far East. On each of her outward voyages she would carry a range of manufactured goods, returning to Northern Europe with cargoes of rubber, cotton and rice.

Her final voyage began from her home port of Oslo on November 19th 1930 under the command of Captain Arthur Wold. Initially she had been instructed to visit the ports of Hamburg, Dunkirk and Rotterdam, picking up a wide range of items that included matches, potassium and other chemicals. In addition, it was at these ports that she was joined by a total of 12 passengers, most of them bound for either Singapore or Shanghai.

Throughout the next six weeks this tramp of the high seas continued to make steady progress. Having left the crowded sea lanes of the industrial north she entered the Mediterranean in December. A brief stop over at Port Said coincided with Christmas, *Tricolor* entering the Suez Canal a few days later. Passing along the Red Sea and Gulf of Aden, she arrived in the Indian Ocean, calling at Colombo early on the morning January 5th.

With her passengers now anxious to see an early completion to this long and obviously tedious voyage, it was agreed that the *Tricolor* would remain here for only a few hours. In fact, her only reason for entering the port of Colombo was to take on a small quantity of fibre and rubber. Fortunately, these particular items were already crated and ready for loading, so the work of transferring the crates was quickly undertaken and the *Tricolor* was again at sea by about midday. Steaming in a southerly direction the twin screwed, oil fired steamer gradually passed along the west coast of the island which was then universally known as Ceylon, but is now Sri Lanka. Towards the middle of the afternoon she appears to have passed through the track of a severe tropical storm, wind and rain forcing the crew to batten down the hatches.

As to precisely what happened next there is a degree of uncertainty. Possibly the vessel was struck by lightning or maybe some of the chemicals began to spill and were somehow ignited. Either way, fire broke out and according to one of the passengers there was a loud bang, followed by a series of smaller explosions.

Flames soon engulfed the entire ship and Captain Wold was left with little alternative but to give the order to abandon ship. As a result most of the crew and all but one of the passengers took to the lifeboats and were soon watching the stricken vessel from a suitably safe distance. On board, Captain Wold remained at the bridge while his wireless operator sent out a frantic SOS.

It was the bravery of these two officers that was responsible for alerting a number of other vessels to the *Tricolor*'s plight. The French liner *Porthos* was on the scene within two hours, taking on board a number of wet and dispirited sailors and passengers. Not to be included amongst the ranks of the saved were all those who had remained on board. A further horrendous explosion had destroyed the entire ship, claiming the lives of both the captain and wireless operator, and those of a fireman and the passenger who had also remained on board.

Doubtless little more would have been heard of this tragedy had it not been for events that were reported to have occurred exactly five years later. On that same day, January 5th, 1936 the British owned freighter *Khosuru*, returning from Bombay to Calcutta, was passing more or less over the site of that fatal explosion. As she did so, according to at least one written account, the *Khosuru* was nearly run down by an apparently deserted ship that had dramatically emerged from beyond a thick curtain of rain.

As this 'ghostlike' vessel crossed the *Khosuru*'s bow she was brought under close observation by all those on the bridge. Among those watching the oncoming vessel was Third Officer G. E. Robinson, the man in charge of the watch. As she slid past, at no more than a cable's length from the *Khosuru*, he was able to read her name. She was the motor vessel *Tricolor*.

Even though she had come so close not one of the *Khosuru*'s crew could see signs of a lookout or even a helmsman at the wheel. It was a narrow shave and Robinson's skipper passed some fairly uncomplimentary remarks about so-called sailors who were unable to keep a proper watch in thick weather.

Maybe those on the bridge would have given little further thought to the matter had it not been for a sudden improvement in the weather. Within a period of only five minutes, according to an account of the incident later written by Robinson, the rain had stopped and the clouds had lifted. Visibility, he stated, had become normal. Proceeding to check the ship's bearings and then fixing their position, Robinson's attention was drawn to a printed symbol on the chart. It was located at a point that was just two miles further back along the track which they had been following. The symbol, which denoted a wreck, was accompanied by a notation: 'Motorship *Tricolor* with cargo of chemicals exploded and sank at this point at 5pm on January 5, 1931.'

Robinson's blood froze and he rushed on to the bridge. 'Where's the *Tricolor*?' he yelled. 'Where's the *Tricolor*?' The Skipper, the Chief Engineer and Robinson all looked around, but there was not a ship in sight, except for a few small native fishing boats. With visibility now good, Robinson estimating it to be about seven miles, the vessel that had just passed them on the port bow should still have been within sight. Instead she had completely disappeared.

Was this seemingly deserted and 'ghostlike' vessel the wraith of the destroyed *Tricolor*? Some would certainly have us believe that this was the case. In the book *From the Devil's Triangle to the Devil's Jaw*, American author Richard Winer assures his readers 'that a later check of records revealed that no vessel with the name *Tricolor* was in the Indian Ocean at all during 1936 or 1937'. While he does not positively state that Robinson sighted a ghost ship, Winer certainly suggests that there is no other plausible alternative.

Unfortunately, in directing his readers towards this particular conclusion, he fails to indicate just which records were checked and by whom. Certainly the search to which he refers could not have been very thorough. Reference to the internationally available *Lloyd's List* for January 1937 reveals that there was, despite Winer's declaration, a cargo ship named *Tricolor* in these very same waters. In fact she was the vessel ordered by Wilhelm Wilhelmsen to replace the one lost in that tragedy off Ceylon. Though slightly larger than the original *Tricolor* she was, nevertheless, a twin screwed oiled fired ship remarkably similar in appearance to the vessel she replaced.

Given that the replacement *Tricolor* was actually in the area on this same day it becomes fairly obvious that this was the vessel actually seen. As to her strange disappearance, this is more likely to be associated with moving banks of rain and the failure of those on board the *Khosuru* to realise that the mist of rain was probably travelling with the *Tricolor*. Even Third Officer Robinson, the main witness to the event, is rather inclined to dismiss the idea of her being a ghost ship. Despite the fact that he was unaware of the replacement *Tricolor* being in these same waters he suggests that her disappearance may well have been the result of light refraction, something which he declares not to be unknown in the tropics.

It seems more than a slight possibility that the vast majority of reported maritime wraiths can probably be explained as a result of similar everyday explanations. Almost certainly the events surrounding a 17th century Dutch ship *Van Holt* provide another example of a supposed wraith that can be more easily explained by recourse to the natural rather than the supernatural.

The *Van Holt* was a two masted square rigger that sailed out of Rotterdam sometime in May 1695. Her delayed return seems to have convinced both the relatives and friends of those on board that she had been unaccountably lost at sea.

Some months later the *Van Holt* could be seen from the Dutch shoreline apparently returning to Rotterdam. At the time a tremendous gale was whipping the seas into a frenzy, forcing the vessel to reduce sail. As the winds continued to increase the *Van Holt* began to heel over, briefly struggled to right herself, then plunged beneath the waves.

Those who had seen and recognised the *Van Holt* firmly believed that they had witnessed the return of her wraith. Dismissing the far more likely possibility of what they had seen being the real *Van Holt*, they chose a far more unlikely explanation. Believing the vessel to have already been wrecked it was comparatively easy for them to assume that this was her apparition. Furthermore, they also believed that the apparition had returned for the single purpose of re-enacting an event that had already taken place in some more distant ocean.

A rather different explanation probably accounts for a number of separate sightings of the five masted *Kobenhavn* following her reported loss. This Danish cadet training ship, the only five masted vessel then in existence, seems to have been overtaken by some unexplained disaster sometime around late December 1928. Possibly her ballast shifted or she struck an iceberg. Either way no satisfactory explanation has ever been given as to why she should suddenly disappear. The ship simply vanished, together with her entire crew of officers and 60 cadets. Here the matter might well have ended had it not been for a series of sightings of a five masted ship during the months following her disappearance. Sightings off the coasts of Peru and Chile, as well as out towards the Easter Islands were assumed by some to be the spectre of the missing *Kobenhavn*.

Surely a far more plausible explanation is that the five masted vessel seen was the real *Kobenhavn*. As each of those sightings came more than a year after the vessel had been officially reported as missing, then it is clear that she had already been overtaken by some kind of disaster which had caused her to be abandoned by her crew. Maybe the *Kobenhavn* had been holed by an iceberg, or perhaps the ballast had shifted. Such a disaster may well have persuaded the crew to take to the lifeboats, convinced that the five-master was about to sink. If either of these events did occur then it is also possible that the *Kobenhavn* either took in less water than at first imagined or miraculously righted herself. Such a turn of events does, at the very least, give a reasonably logical explanation for the continued existence of a five masted sailing ship in the Pacific Ocean during this period. Eventually, of course, the abandoned hulk would have succumbed to the elements. With her sails hoisted she would have been easy prey to the first hurricane to catch up with her, but until that happened she would have sailed on without a human soul on board.

However, not all reported sightings of phantom ships are so easily explained. Consider for instance the variety of sightings that have been reported from around the coastline of North America.

Off San Francisco the old clipper *Tennessee* was at one time frequently reported attempting to enter Golden Gate Harbour. Running for port with all her sails set she seems never to have reached her apparent destintion. Instead, as she came level with Line Port she would simply disappear, only to re-appear further out to sea.

Around Orr's Island, Maine the incredible sight of a ship manned by skeletons is supposed to appear, while the coast of New Hampshire is said to be haunted by a 19th century sailing ship named *White Rover*. Further north, residents of Nova Scotia's Chester Bay have occasionally seen an ancient French caravel. A second Nova Scotia haunting involves the *St Martins*, engulfed in flames. She is occasionally seen in the Bay of Fundy.

At the mouth of the St Lawrence an ancient sailing ship is supposed to appear once every year. Starting out as a ball of fire, it gradually takes on the shape of a sailing ship. According to tradition this vessel is said to be the *Packet Light*, but no date is given for her loss. In New Brunswick, Chaleur Bay is said to be haunted by a British man-o'-war, sent there during the reign of Queen Anne. Unfortunately my own search of naval records has failed to produce a vessel lost in that area during the early years of the 18th century.

The most unusual reported sighting of a ghost ship in American waters took place during the summer of 1967. The witnesses were a small family group engaged on a yachting cruise off the New England coast. It appears that early one morning while they were some 220 miles off Cape Cod, they were suddenly confronted by a huge submarine in the process of surfacing. Painted in white along the side of the conning tower was the name *Thresher*.

At first the occupants of the yacht were not particularly concerned by the presence of this vessel. Although it might have proved a hazard if it had been under them at the time of surfacing, it was at this moment some distance away. But as they watched the submarine complete its manouvering it became apparent that she was in some difficulty. They noticed that it moved rather sluggishly. Then they saw that the submarine had a long sharp gash running down the side. In fact, they found it difficult to understand how the submarine was retaining her buoyancy. Yet, somewhat surprisingly, two of the submarine's crew who could also be seen, were not the least concerned with the vessel's plight. Instead, they seemed to be more interested in studying the occupants of the yacht through binoculars.

Suddenly the gash seemed to take effect. But in a rather strange and unexpected way. Without warning the vessel slowly began to rise into the air. Having somehow levitated itself a few feet above the ocean, it suddenly collapsed upon itself and disappeared into the sea!

Telling only a few people of their unusual experience those on board the yacht decided to carry out a little background research. To start with they decided to see if there had ever been a submarine with the name *Thresher*. To their amazement they discovered that just such a submarine had once existed. This was the *USS Thresher*. Only two years earlier this particular vessel had hit the news headlines when she mysteriously disappeared while on a post-refit diving trial. At the time it had been considered possible that she had suffered a severe electrical fault causing complete loss of control.

Thresher's last known position, was reported as being just 220 miles off Cape Cod. In other words, more or less the same position as the strangely behaving apparition witnessed during that summer of 1967.

In recounting this particular story of a spectral ship it must be mentioned that at least one piece of information lacks credibility. If the vessel seen was the the true wraith of *Thresher* then her name would not have appeared on the conning tower or any other part of the vessel. US submarines of the 'Thresher' class (renamed 'Permit' class following the loss of *Thresher*) simply carry a pennant number painted in white. In *Thresher*'s case the number was 593.

Apart from the waters surrounding the coastline of North America, there are a great many other seaways that can lay claim to their own spectral ships. Returning briefly to the Indian Ocean (where the two *Tricolors* once sailed) there is a mystical legend declaring that a fleet of small boats could be regularly seen passing through the Straits of Sundra. Supposedly these are the various doppelgangers of numerous small boats that tried, unsuccessfully, to escape the great tidal wave brought about by the eruption of Krakatoa in 1883.

In the seas that skirt the coast of China it is said that a ghost ship of a 15th century pirate is occasionally glimpsed. Among those said to be on board is the abducted daughter of a Japanese nobleman.

Another area of the world haunted by a spectral ship is the Mediterranean. Here an ancient galley carries a phantom crew long since ravaged by plague. The legend tells of how the various city ports that surround the Mediterranean refused to allow this plague-ridden vessel sanctuary. As a result those on board were condemned to sail the Middle Seas for all time.

Around the coasts of Great Britain there are a myriad of similar stories and half forgotten myths. While lazing on the popular summer-time beaches of Brighton in Sussex it is believed possible to see a 10th century galley. According to ancient tradition the vessel, which is said to be the *Nicholas* sunk with all hands when returning from a pilgrimage to Constantinople.

But it is the English West Country that boasts more legends of ghost ships than any other area. There seems to be hardly a

The United States submarine *Thresher*. Her wraith was reported during the summer of 1967. Note her pennant number which clearly appears on the side of her conning tower. [United States Naval Institute]

single cove or inlet that is without its ghost ship. A great number of these stories concern the annual return of a lost vessel to the village from which the majority of its crew must have once hailed. Some of these stories appear to be soundly rooted, the vessel, if not the doppelganger, having once existed. Others however are complete inventions and have not even the evidence of an original ship to support the story.

One tale from the West Country is of a spectral lugger which appears off the Lizard. According to tradition she re-enacts events that led up to her loss some hundred or more years ago. Almost certainly this is one of the many ghost ships of Cornwall that has some sort of basis in fact. It must be remembered that there were a great many fishing boats that set out from these waters, with large numbers failing to return. As to which of these is the spectral lugger of Cornwall only the crew themselves could now give us the answer.

A somewhat more involved story comes from another Cornish port, St Ives. During an earlier century a gale damaged ship was seen approaching the port. In the hope of rendering assistance a group of local men set off in a small flat bottomed fishing boat. Drawing level with the stricken vessel they called for a rope to be thrown down. This was done, but as soon as one of the would-be rescuers grabbed the rope both it and the ship vanished. All were convinced that they had seen the spectre of a previously wrecked ship. But they were wrong!

Some twelve hours later, with a gale having now whipped the waves into a frothing cauldron, another vessel appeared off St Ives. It was the *Neptune*, a vessel identical to the ship previously seen. She was failing to make any headway against the severe winds and watchers on shore saw the *Neptune* gradually forced over. With her storm sails dipping beneath the waves she had no chance of recovery. Slowly she slid beneath the water. It was then that those on shore realised that this was exactly the same spot where the earlier ship had so dramatically disappeared!

While evidence for spectral ships around the coasts of

Devon and Cornwall is sometimes a little vague, firmer ground exists when it comes to the Goodwin Sands. Lying close to the entrance of the English Channel and approximately four miles east of Deal in Kent, this extensive sand bank has, over the years, literally claimed thousands of ships.

One startling piece of evidence for a ghost ship on the Sands comes from George Carter, a former keeper on the Goodwin lightship. Carter, in a later published book, describes an event that he witnessed during the first week of 1947. On that occasion he watched a steamer directly approaching the Sands, the vessel failing to heed warning signals to alter course. A squall of driving snow prevented those on board the lightship seeing the vessel's exact fate, but a series of emergency rockets, 'pale and feeble over the Goodwins', were seen coming from a point close to where the steamer had last been seen. Answering rockets were fired from the lightship and the Ramsgate lifeboat was launched, but despite a thorough search nothing resembling the lost ship was discovered.

George Carter, who later wrote a complete history of the Goodwin Sands, was convinced that the vessel he had seen was the *Violet*. This was a former Royal Dover Steam Packet that had travelled the same course exactly ninety years earlier. Eighteen crew and one passenger had been drowned when the captain lost his bearings and managed to run his ship on to the sands. At the time the weather was not dissimilar to that witnessed by Carter during the first week of 1947.

The most famous of the phantom ships associated with the Goodwin Sands is the *Lady Lovibund*, a schooner outward bound from London, which was wrecked on the Sands on February 13th 1748. Since that time a number of interesting stories have attached themselves to the vessel.

According to one widely held belief the ship was deliberately steered on to the Sands by her first mate, John Rivers. However, such a suggestion must remain unsubstantiated, there being no survivors from the wreck.

It appears that Rivers was jealous of Simon Peel, the schooner's master. The two men had been rivals in love and Simon Peel had eventually won the desired female. In fact, the wedding had only just taken place, with many of the guests and the new Mrs Peel having come on the voyage in order to continue celebrating the wedding.

As for the phantom re-appearance of the *Lady Lovibund*, this is supposed to take place on each 50th anniversary of her loss. Accordingly, it was on February 13th 1798 that the apparition of the *Lady Lovibund* was first reported by Captain James Westlake on board the *Edenbridge*. He reported a three masted schooner bearing down on his own ship. As she passed by he distinctly heard sounds of merry making. Later Westlake discovered that the crew of a lugger had also seen this same schooner smash into the Sands and, approaching the scene of what they assumed to be a major tragedy, they found absolutely nothing.

Other sightings of the *Lady Lovibund* seem to have taken place during February 1848 and then again in February 1898. On both occasions boats were launched for the purpose of carrying out a rescue but no trace of a wreck could be found.

As for 1948 there does not appear to have been a reported sighting on that anniversary, although a remarkable suggestion has been made. According to a view current at the time, the loss of the *Silvia Onorato*, an Italian freighter claimed by the Sands in January of that year, might have been a live sacrifice demanded by the *Lady Lovibund*. After all, the *Silvia Onorato* did strike the Sands close to the day when the *Lady Lovibund* should have made her re-appearance. But if you believe that, then I am inclined to suggest that you might believe anything.

In all there are at least eight vessels lost on the Goodwin Sands for which claims of a spectral reappearance have been made. Amongst this list of ships is one from the Great Storm of 1703. On the night of November 25th/26th of that year a severe hurricane claimed a great many ships along the English coastline. Among them were several vessels from a squadron of warships that were then heading for the royal dockyard and naval base at Chatham. When the storm struck they were approaching the Sands and only a few were given the chance of survival.

In the event, the Sands claimed four of these vessels. Amongst them was the 3rd rate man-o'-war *Northumberland*. She allegedly appeared in spectral form exactly 50 years later. According to the log of an East Indiaman: 'At ten of the clock this day (November 28th, 1753), while riding out bad weather off Goodwins . . . an armed frigate came driving down on my ship, her mast gone, her decks and hull in fearful shape'. The writer of this particular entry continues by declaring that the frigate appeared to be quite unmanageable and was forced along at a pace faster than the wind could possibly have achieved. In seeing this, and how the ship even had the ability to run against the wind, the writer concluded that the vessel was a phantom.

Other ghost ships that have made appearances on the Goodwin Sands include a Spanish galleon that grounds on the Sands before breaking into pieces. Her particular apparition is accompanied by the booming of guns.

Another more recent Goodwin Sands phantom ship is the *Montrose*. She originally struck the Sands in December 1914. At the time the *Montrose*, a former Canadian liner, was already at the end of her sea going days. Having been filled with cement, it was intended that she should be sunk at the mouth of the River Thames as a war time blockship. That the *Montrose* escaped this particular indignity was the result of a sudden storm that struck the vessel while she was moored in Dover Harbour. She was driven completely out of the harbour and crashed on to the Sands at a point about one and a half miles north-west of the East Goodwin Lightship. Unlike many of the Goodwin Sands apparitions however, the re-appearance of the *Montrose* is a little less predictable, her last sighting having taken place in 1965.

The Goodwin Sands claims yet another victim. A dangerous
sand bank that lies in the midst of the English Channel, it can
claim a record number of ghost ships.

As already mentioned, the claims for phantom ships on the Goodwin Sands are fairly extensive. However, it is unwise to accept all of these stories without careful thought to possible alternative explanations.

Some accounts claim yet one more spectral ship from that ill-fated naval squadron in the Great Storm of 1703. This was the *Shrewsbury*, another 3rd rate. But a check on the movement of ships on that particular night reveals that *Shrewsbury* was fortunate enough to arrive safely in Chatham. She subsequently had a long career which eventually ended with her being broken up at Portsmouth in 1749. In the light of this information it seems highly unlikely that any force, either in heaven or on earth, could possibly have wished a return of the vessel to the Goodwin Sands.

8

The *Ellen Austin* Mystery

When trying to put together a book of true ghost stories there is always pressure upon the writer to either exaggerate the basic story or to make certain assumptions. The result is that a fairly mediocre or everyday event can, in the hands of some authors, be turned into something that sounds both bizarre and inexplicable. The classic example of this, when it comes to phantom stories associated with the high seas, is the variety of versions of an encounter that took place between the *Ellen Austin* and a derelict ship sometime during the year 1881.

Over the years, so it would appear, the basic story of this encounter has been used by a number of writers, each one seemingly in competition to produce a new or unexpected twist to a story that, in itself, may not even be true. As a result a fairly interesting story, with only a slight hint of a connection with the world of the supernatural, has become so distorted as to leave no alternative explanation.

The first traceable reference to the *Ellen Austin* story appears in a small book entitled *Stargazer Talks*, published in 1944 and written by Commander R. T. Gould, a retired British naval officer who became a well-known broadcaster. Based on a talk that Gould had previously given some nine years earlier, the reference to the *Ellen Austin* appears at the end of a section dedicated to the *Mary Celeste* and other ships found similarly abandoned. It is worth quoting Gould's reference to the *Ellen Austin* in full:

Last, and queerest of all, comes the case of the abandoned derelict, in seaworthy condition, which the British ship *Ellen Austin* encountered, in mid-Atlantic, in the year 1881. She put a small prize crew on board the stranger, with instructions to make for St John's, Newfoundland, where she was bound herself.

The two ships parted company in foggy weather – but a few days later they met again. And the strange derelict was once more deserted. Like their predecessors, the prize crew had vanished – for ever.

Although an unusual story, the *Ellen Austin*'s loss of her prize crew need not take us into the realms of the supernatural. There are many possibilities for her having been abandoned. To start with, the vessel may not have been as totally sea-worthy as suggested. The prize crew may, in fact, have dis-covered something seriously wrong with the vessel and, like her original crew and for the same reason, departed her for their own safety. Alternatively, they could have been attacked by pirates and forced to join another ship. Either suggestion is as likely as the crew having been spirited off by some unknown and unimaginable force from the spirit world.

Of course, Gould gives sufficient clues for the entire story to be verified and possibly solved. Apart from naming the ship he gives the year and an approximate position. Given that the encounter with the derelict was somewhat unusual, it would, most assuredly, have been reported in a number of newspapers. However, a search through the files of the *The Times* and the specialist shipping newspaper *Lloyd's List*, together with the Newfoundland based *Royal Gazette and Newfoundland Advertiser*, failed to bring forward any refer-ence to this mid-Atlantic encounter. In addition, the fairly complete records of the World Ship Society offer no refer-ences to any vessel having been named *Ellen Austin* during the period to which Gould refers.

Indeed, this inability to uncover any further background information to the story is probably an even greater mystery. It leaves anyone wishing to make greater use of this story slightly stranded. For my part, when I started writing this particular book, I was very keen on using the Ellen Austin story, but I also wished to find out more about the ship, her crew and that mid-Atlantic encounter. While there was only the merest hint of a supernatural connection, there was always the possibility of Gould having missed some important fact or there being other similarly strange things occurring. However, unable to pursue the story any further, the project was temporarily abandoned.

To my surprise however, I noted that a number of other writers had seemingly discovered a great deal more. In a number of books, all written after the publication of Gould's *Stargazer Talks*, it is possible to discover a range of interesting facts about the *Ellen Austin* and her mid-Atlantic encounter. The least sensational of these accounts has the ship, heading not for Newfoundland but for New York, having departed from Liverpool. Similarly, another account tells us that the first encounter was 600 miles off the coast of Ireland and the second encounter 300 miles off Sandy Hook.

These additions to the tale are fairly tame when compared with a crop of books that associate the *Ellen Austin* with the mysterious happenings associated with a rather imprecise area of water known as 'The Bermuda Triangle'. Again such books purport to offer a wealth of additional detail. In one version of the story, the *Ellen Austin*'s destination has become Boston, while the derelict is said to have come from one of the South American ports. These accounts, however, tend to be a little more contradictory as to where the *Ellen Austin* first encountered the derelict, it being variously suggested, according to the book read, that it was either west of the Azores or somewhere between the Bahamas and Bermuda.

In associating the *Ellen Austin* with the 'Bermuda Triangle' saga, a number of other interesting additions creep into the story. Most incredible is that Gould's original story is somewhat extended. While Gould ended with the first prize crew having 'vanished for ever', some of these writers introduce a second prize crew. Not surprisingly, this second group are most unwilling to join the vessel but are 'finally persuaded' by the captain's persistence 'to man the mysterious and apparently dangerous ship'. In most accounts concerned with the 'Bermuda Triangle' the two ships remain together for a few days but then, either as a result of a squall or through being 'engulfed in the watery haze', those on board the *Ellen Austin* lose sight of their charge. Returning to the spot where the derelict was last seen, the ocean is found to be empty. The prize ship had simply spirited away a second crew. For one author, a comparison is suggested between the abandoned ship and a trap, 'if the whole idea were not so *outré*'.

Now, in reading these additional accounts, I was intrigued to know where these particular authors had got their information. Fortunately, I also discovered that this aspect of the story had already been examined by Larry Kusche. In his own book, *The Bermuda Triangle Mystery – Solved*, and in a series of more detailed essays, Kusche concluded that these additions leaned upon the fanciful rather than the factual.

To begin with, he too had started with the files of various 19th century newspapers. In his case, he concentrated on the indices of the *New York Times* and *The Times* of London together with a microfilm of *The Newfoundlander*. He examined the latter, column by column, for the entire period from January 1st 1881 through to mid-1882. According to Kusche's later summary of this research, 'it was an extremely tedious job – examining small, dim print of often headlineless articles – that took several hours an evening for almost a month'. Noting that St. John's was far from being the centre of the world at that time, he indicated that any possible newsworthy event was always recorded. 'Yet, there was not one mention of the *Ellen Austin*, or of any similar incident involving a ship of any name, in that year and a half'.

Shortly after he had finished his research, a further account of the *Ellen Austin* incident appeared. This was by far the most detailed, and gave a new port of destination, Boston, together with an exact date of the first sighting, August 20th 1881. As with all previous accounts of the story, no source was given. Kusche, not unnaturally, was determined to check out this new version of events. To begin with, he again turned to the *New York Times* and *The Times*, before directing himself to the Boston newspapers. Again, not one single reference was found to the incident, nor any reference to the *Ellen Austin* even having arrived at this port during the late-summer early-autumn period

Kusche's time did not appear to be entirely wasted, however. He did at least find reference to a vessel named *Ellen Austin* in records at the Boston Public Library, so proving she did at least exist.

The point of all this, even given that the *Ellen Austin* was no mere fictional vessel, is that all too often the desire to produce a good sea story leads to the type of exaggeration and clear distortion that has resulted in the complete confusion of Gould's original account. It seems unlikely that any of these writers had come across a hitherto undiscovered source. Certainly none of them indicate this to be the case in their various given accounts or as part of a bibliography and which suggests the possibility that the additional material has simply been invented. This, so it would appear, happens frequently.

Casual readers, are left in a position where they are completely unable to distinguish the amount of fact from fiction. As a result they must accept on trust a highly sensationalised account. In such stories numerous suppositional links are made with the supernatural but, in reality, they simply cannot be substantiated!

9

The Headless Mate

The port of Bathurst, situated within the Canadian province of New Brunswick, offers the ghost hunter a truly sensational story: a phantom of the high seas par excellence. It is a tale of the supernatural that leaves one with a feeling of real horror.

On a cold and silent night, sometime towards the end of the 19th century, two watchmen were reliably reported to have seen a most fearsome apparition. It was something that neither man could ever wish to see again. But until their dying days it was something that they would never forget. Like some hideous nightmare it constantly returned to their thoughts. What they saw, if you dare to believe it, was the figure of a headless man. And, to those who were confronted by this terrifying sight, there was an overwhelming feeling that it meant to do them harm. Both men truly believed that their lives were in danger and that they were unlikely to escape.

Fortunately for those still living in Bathurst, this headless ghost never appears to have strayed from the *Squando*, a vessel which has long since disappeared from any of the world's shipping lists. A search through the records however will show that this particular vessel did at one time most certainly exist. She was built by C. Sorrell of St John's, New Brunswick, a three masted barque of 1,220 tons, a type regarded in her day as a useful workhorse by any small company trading the oceans.

To begin with the *Squando* appears to have had a reasonably uneventful career. Mostly to be found in the Atlantic, she frequently brought cargoes into the various New Brunswick ports, but was also a regular visitor to New York, Boston and Baltimore. At some time, indeed, she even rounded the Horn, taking materials to the rapidly expanding West Coast towns that included San Francisco and Los Angeles.

It was during the 1880s that the first of a series of tragic events struck the vessel. This may have been partly due to the difficulties she encountered in coming round Cape Horn. Leastways, an argument certainly erupted between the master and the ship's mate. Some suggest that this clash involved the captain's wife. On this voyage, so it would appear, the captain had decided to take her on board. Possibly she had expressed an interest in seeing the fabled sight of those mushrooming new cities that looked across the Pacific Ocean.

During the long voyage it seems likely that the mate began taking an interest in the captain's wife. Perhaps they were often left alone together. Maybe the captain caught the pair of them in a compromising situation. The mate might well have thought his advances were being encouraged, but this was not the wife's version of events. She told her husband that she had been deeply insulted and that the mate had forced himself upon her. The captain became absolutely livid and in no mood to forgive his second in command. He set about planning his revenge.

When the *Squando* eventually came to anchor in the port of San Francisco both the captain and his wife stole up on the mate. The captain, seizing the man bodily, drew out a hideously sharp knife and sliced off his head. It was a gory affair. Blood saturated the ship's timbers. Not surprisingly, both the captain and his wife were arrested and a new captain took charge of the *Squando*.

Perhaps it was the bloodstained deck or simply the restless nature of a murdered man. Either way, the *Squando* failed to return to that earlier period of tranquillity. From now on nothing seemed to go right for those who served on board the vessel. Over the following years there were at least three other deaths on board the vessel. In each case, strange to relate, the victim was the captain.

It was almost as if the ship, or something on board her, had an intense hatred of the man in command. First to die was the replacement captain who had come on board at San Francisco. He lasted but a few months. The crew, for some reason, mutinied. Something had got into them and they rose up and killed the captain. The result was more arrests and the need for another captain.

The new captain and his successor, were also short-lived. Both died in the course of their duties, neither of them able to come to terms with the *Squando* and her rapidly growing reputation for evil. During this period ownership of the vessel also changed hands, with the vessel eventually flying the Norwegian flag.

As news got round the shipping world, it became increasingly difficult to find a crew who were prepared to board the fated ship. On her final arrival at Bathurst those on board deserted and no one else would join her. The ship had been left stranded.

At first, a couple of watchmen were appointed to look after her. Both lasted just one night. According to Frederick George Lee, a one time collector of weird and strange stories connected with the supernatural, neither watchmen was prepared to remain on board for a second night. 'They asserted that they saw a headless man walking about in the cabin,' Frederick Lee relates. 'That handspikes were flying round the deck, hurled by invisible hands; that their bed clothes were pulled off them; that a cold clammy hand was laid on their faces...'

Certainly, the two watchmen were terrified. Bringing the matter to the attention of their employer, the Norwegian consul, they even told him of voices insisting that they should leave the ship. Doubtless, the consul would merely have dismissed the entire matter had it not been for the fact that the story as told by the two watchmen was confirmed by others. According to several other individuals, all of whom were unknown to the watchmen, they too had boarded the vessel and encountered a similar barrage of flying implements and whispering voices. As Frederick Lee adds, it was this confirmation of the watchmen's experience 'that led to the immediate abandonment of a vessel of very considerable value.'

Was it, so it must now be asked, something to do with the murder of the former mate back in San Francisco? After all, it was a headless ghost that had been reported and the mate had certainly been decapitated.

As with any ghost story it is impossible to be absolutely definite. But the evidence certainly points in that direction. Putting aside the beheading, it should also be noted that the problems on board the *Squando* began shortly after the mate's death. This man, having died in such an horrific manner while on board, may well have decided in the spirit world to take his revenge. At the very least, he was not going to make it easy for any one else who intended making a living on board the *Squando*.

Furthermore, the mate, or whoever else this headless ghost may have been, was no lover of authority. In nearly all cases, so it would appear, this spirit seemed to reserve its full venom for those who took command. No captain, as others had quickly realised, would be safe on that particular vessel. For this reason she never took on another crew and ended her days as an abandoned hulk in that New Brunswick port.

10
The Legend of the Damned

The legend of a ship and her crew, condemned to sail the world's oceans for eternity, is a frequently repeated story. Versions are to be found within such widespread cultures as those of southern India, mainland China, north America and western Europe. In each case, either the captain of the ship, or a member of his crew, has performed such a ghastly deed that no other punishment appeared suitable, the transgressor so evil that death would be only a mild retribution for the crime committed.

Most enduring of these legends is that of the 'Flying Dutchman'. Although several versions of the story are known to exist, the one most popularly accepted is that written down by Frenchman Auguste Jal sometime around the year 1832. Appearing in his *Scènes de la Vie Maritime*, it is worth quoting in full:

> 'Sometime in the past there was a ship's captain who feared neither God nor the saints. He is said to be a Dutchman, but I am not sure, nor does it greatly matter, from where he came. He happened once to be making a voyage to the South. All went well until he came near the Cape of Good Hope, where he ran into a head wind strong enough to blow the horns off a bull.
>
> 'The ship was in considerable danger and everyone began to say to the Captain, "Captain, we must turn back. If you insist on continuing to try to round the Cape we shall be lost. We shall

inevitably perish and there is no priest on board to give us absolution.''

'But the Captain laughed at the fears of his crew and passengers, and began to sing songs so horrible and blasphemous that they might well have attracted the lightning to his mast a hundred times over. Then he calmly smoked his pipe and drank his beer as though he were seated in a tavern. His people renewed their demands to turn the ship around, but the more they demanded the more obstinate he became. His masts were broken, his sails torn and near useless, but he merely laughed as a man might who had a piece of good news.

'So the Captain continued to treat with equal contempt the violence of the storm, the protests of the crew and the fears of the passengers, and when his men attempted to force him to make for the shelter of a bay, he flung the leader overboard. But even as he did so the clouds parted and a ghostly presence alighted on the quarter deck. The presence is said to have been the Almighty himself. The crew and passengers were stricken with fear, but the captain went on smoking his pipe, and did not even touch his cap when the presence addressed him.

'"Captain," said the presence, "you are very stubborn."

'"And you are a rascal," cried the captain. "Who wants a peaceful passage? I don't. I'm asking nothing from you, so clear out of this unless you want your brains blown out."

'The presence gave no answer other than a shrug of the shoulders. The captain then picked up a pistol, cocked it and fired. The bullet, instead of racing towards its target, misfired and scratched the captain's hand. The captain's fury knew no bounds. He leapt up to strike the presence in the face, but his arm dropped limply to his side as though paralysed. In his rage he cursed and blasphemed and called the presence all sorts of terrible names.

'The presence then addressed the captain, "From now on you are accursed, condemned to sail for ever. You will be allowed no anchorage or port of any kind. You shall have neither beer nor tobacco. Gall shall be your drink and red hot iron your meat. Of your crew, your cabin boy alone shall remain with you; horns shall grow out of his forehead, and he shall have the muzzle of a tiger and skin tougher than that of a dogfish".

'The captain groaned, but the presence continued, "It shall ever be your watch, and when you wish, you will not be able to sleep, for directly you close your eyes a sword shall pierce your body. And since it is your delight to torment sailors, you shall torment them."

'At this, the captain smiled.

'"For you shall be the evil spirit of the sea," the presence continued. "You shall travel all latitudes without rest and your ship shall bring misfortune to all who sight it".

'"Amen to that!" shouted the captain with a smirk upon his face.

'"And on the day of atonement, the Devil shall claim you".

'"A fig for the Devil!" was the captain's reply.

'The presence disappeared. On board the ship, the Dutchman was alone, except for the cabin boy who now had horns and the face of a tiger. The rest of the crew had vanished.

'From that day forward the Flying Dutchman has sailed the seas, and it is his pleasure to torment poor mariners. He sets them a false course, sending them towards uncharted shoals. He turns their wine sour and all their food into beans. Sometimes he sends letters on board the ships he meets, and if the captain tries to read them he is lost. Or an empty boat will draw along side the Phantom ship

and disappear, a sure sign of ill-fortune. He can
change at will the appearance of his ship, so as not
to be recognised. Around him he has also collected
a crew as cursed as himself. All the criminals,
pirates and cowards of the sea.'

There is, of course, one important detail missing from Jal's
account, the captain's name. At no point does Jal attempt to
indicate who this evil, raving lunatic might have been. Others
however, have not been slow with presenting likely candi-
dates. One who neatly fits all of the stated facts is a certain
Cornelius Vanderdecken.

This particular individual, captain of a Dutch East Indiaman, had the same fiery temper and disregard for human life
as that already described by Jal. More important, as a possible candidate for this unenviable condition of eternal life,
Vanderdecken frequently sailed the southern oceans, passing
the Cape of Good Hope two or three times in each year.
Concerned only with making a rapid passage, it is said that
Vanderdecken never shortened sail and frequently defiled
the name of the Almighty.

The name of another Dutch sea captain, Bernard Fokke,
has also been put forward as the original 'Flying Dutchman'.
He, too, had a raging temper and little concern for those who
were unfortunate enough to serve under him. Often making
the passage from Batavia to Holland in 90 days, the storms
around the Cape of Good Hope were of as little consequence
to him as a breeze rippling the waters of a secluded village
pond.

According to tradition Fokke was so concerned that each of
his voyages should be made in record time that he entered
into a pact with the Devil. The exact terms go unrecorded, but
it is suggested that the Devil gave him one very useful piece of
equipment. So as to allow Fokke to cram on a maximum
amount of sail the Devil turned his timber masts into iron. As
a result a full suit of sails could be raised in even the severest

of storms. However, Fokke appears to have fallen out with his mentor. The result was that on the next occsion when he rounded the Cape of Good Hope the Devil once again boarded the Dutchman's ship. Determined to punish his former supplicant, he bestowed upon Fokke the terrors of eternally sailing the world's oceans.

Now whether the 'Flying Dutchman' is Cornelius Vanderdecken or Bernard Fokke would appear to be of little consequence. After all, the idea of being so condemned is about as believable as the voyage of the mythical *Argo* under the command of Jason. However, the difficulty in simply dismissing the legend of the 'Flying Dutchman' is that just such a vessel has frequently been seen. Sometimes it is in the southern oceans, approaching the Cape of Good Hope, but other times it has been sighted in more northerly latitudes. Furthermore, ill-luck often befalls those ships coming into contact with this eternal sailer of the high seas.

The most famous sighting of the 'Flying Dutchman' was made by no less a person than a future King of England. In 1881 Prince George later to become King George V, was serving as a midshipman on board HMS *Inconstant*. On July 11th with the vessel on passage between Melbourne and Sydney, the Prince was midshipman of the Morning Watch.

To begin with, it proved a fairly uneventful turn of duty. The heavily armed steam frigate *Inconstant* was sailing in company with the corvettes *Cleopatra* and *Tourmaline*, with the endless monotony broken only by the need to keep a wary eye on the position of these two other vessels. Then, as the early morning sun began to break over the horizon, something quite startling occurred. For posterity the future king recorded the event in his private journal:

> July 11th, 1881. At 4am the 'Flying Dutchman' crossed our bows. A strange red light, as of a phantom ship all aglow, in the midst of which light the mast, spars, and sails of a brig two hundred

A rare early photograph of the future George V of England. He is standing in the centre of the group immediately behind Queen Alexandra (seated second right). As a young midshipman on board the *Inconstant*, the prince reported seeing the 'Flying Dutchman'. This photograph was taken on board HMS *Thrush*, his first commission.

yards distant stood out in strong relief as she came up on the port bow. The look-out man on the forecastle reported her as close on the port bow, where also the officer of the watch from the bridge clearly saw her, as did also the quarterdeck midshipman, who was sent forward at once to the forecastle; but on arriving there, no vestige nor any sign whatever of any material ship was to be seen either near or right away to the horizon, the night being clear and sea calm. Thirteen persons saw her, but whether it was 'Van Diemen' or the 'Flying Dutchman', or who else, must remain unknown. The *Tourmaline* and *Cleopatra*, who were sailing on our starboard bow, flashed to ask whether we had seen the strange light.

It was soon after the sighting of this strange spectral ship that ill-luck began to dog H.M.S. *Inconstant*. Again, it is worth referring to the notes that Prince George made at the time:

At 10.45 am the ordinary seaman who had this morning reported the 'Flying Dutchman' fell from the fore-topmast cross-trees and was smashed to atoms. At 4.15 pm, after quarters, we hove to with the headyards aback, and he was buried at sea. He was a smart royalyardman, and one of the most promising hands in the ship, and everyone feels sad at his loss. At the next port the Admiral also was smitten down.

A possible further sighting of the 'Flying Dutchman' came just two years later. In his book, *The Roaring Forties and After*, D. J. Munro relates an unusual experience that took place when he was just 17 years old and third mate on a New Zealand bound clipper. He tells of how the weather threatened and started to blow up as for a storm:

To windward we saw a large ship standing on the same course, evidently a 'Blue Nose' packet (Nova Scotia or Yankee). The mist was in patches and

when it cleared off nothing could be seen of the
ship. What became of her was much discussed on
board. Every man in the watch saw her repeatedly,
so there was no doubt as to her being there. The
weather was not bad and there was no visible
reason why she should have foundered. She might
have altered her course, but there was no apparent
reason why she should do this.

Normally, ill-fortune accompanies any sightings of the 'Flying
Dutchman'. On this occasion not only did Munro's vessel
survive, but Munro himself lived to tell the tale. Perhaps,
therefore, the vessel sighed was not the Dutchman, flying or
otherwise!

A more definite sighting took place in January 1911. Leastways, some of the crew of the whaling steamer *Orkney Belle*
certainly thought they had come upon the legendary Vanderdecken. The only problem was that the *Orkney Belle* was five
miles off Reykjavik, an area of the world's oceans not
normally associated with the travels of the 'Flying Dutchman'. An account of this episode was subsequently given to
the London *Daily News* by the *Orkney Belle*'s second mate:

> The captain and I were on the bridge and a thin
> mist swirled over everything. Suddenly this thin
> mist thinned out, leaving visibility easy. To our
> mutual horror and surprise, a sailing vessel loomed
> up virtually head on. I rammed the helm hard
> aport and we seemed to escape collision by a hair's
> breadth.
>
> Meantime, the captain signalled dead slow to
> the engine room. Then, with startling suddenness
> old Anderson, the carpenter, bawled out: 'The
> Flying Dutchman!'
>
> The captain and I scoffed at him, for we thought
> that oft-fabled ship existed in the minds of only
> superstitious sailors.
>
> As the strange vessel slowly slid alongside within

a stone's throw, we noticed with amazement that her sails were billowing, yet there was no wind at all. She was a replica of a barque I once saw in a naval museum – high poop and carved stern – but we could not observe her name.

Meantime, practically all the crew rushed to the ship's side, some in terror, but unable to resist their curiosity. Not a soul was to be seen aboard this strange vessel, not a ripple did her bows make.

Then, like a silver bell, so sweet was the tone, three bells sounded, as if from the bows of the phantom ship, and as if in answer to a signal, the craft heeled to starboard and disappeared into the fog which was returning.

I sailed with the old *Orkney Belle* several times, but never saw the queer old ship again. If any of my old ship mates on the *Orkney Belle* are still alive, I am sure they will corroborate my statement.

In fact, sightings of the 'Flying Dutchman' are not particularly unusual. Newspapers frequently carry references to the vessel, with several reported sightings having occurred in both more recent years and at various times throughout the previous century. A spate of sightings, for instance, were reported by U-boat commanders during the Second World War. This fact was verified by Admiral Donitz who, from 1935 onwards, was in charge of German submarine operations:

> Certain of my U-boat crews claimed they saw the Flying Dutchman or some other so-called phantom ship on their tours of duty east of Suez. When they returned to their base the men said they preferred facing the combined strength of Allied warships in the North Atlantic than know the terror a second time of being confronted by a phantom vessel.

It was the passengers and crew of an American ship who are described as having had the least enviable of all experiences

111

connected with the 'Flying Dutchman'. This was the *General Grant*, a three master of 1,200 tons and registered at the port of Boston. Sleek and exceptionally fast, she was most frequently employed on the profitable trade route between London and Australia.

At the beginning of May 1866 she embarked upon her last ever voyage. Leaving Hobson's Bay, Melbourne on the 4th she headed out in a south-easterly direction, her immediate destination being Cape Horn. According to her manifest she carried a mixed cargo that consisted of a variety of animal skins, horns and 2,057 bales of wool. In addition she also carried a total of 46 passengers (13 in her first class cabins and 33 in the second and third class areas). A number of these passengers were returning gold prospectors a fact which, as events turned out, was to prove somewhat fortuitous. It was the experience that some of them had gained from living a rugged, open air existence that was to ensure the survival of at least a few of their fellow passengers.

The first week of the voyage presented few problems. A light westerly wind pushed the ship forward at a steady pace, allowing her passengers confidently to expect an uninterrupted journey home. But matters did not remain so. At the start of the second week the weather took a decided turn for the worse. With the barometer falling and clouds beginning to thicken, it became increasingly difficult to plot their position. However, the real problem was that of the wind which had now considerably slackened. Nothing more than a light breeze from the north-west, it was too weak to provide the vessel with any hope of fighting a strong north-westerly current. This resulted in the ill-fated *General Grant* being pushed further and further away from the normal trade routes. With the vessel's master, Captain William Loughlin, unable to take a sun shot due to dense cloud, he became unaware of just how far off course the vessel had begun to drift.

On May 13th the *General Grant* passed the appropriately named Disappointment Island, one of a number of extremely inhospitable islands to be found in this part of the Southern Ocean. It was completely uninhabited and due to its distance from normal trade routes only the occasional whaler or lost merchantman ever came within hailing distance of this or other islands that made up the Auckland group.

As the *General Grant* continued to be pushed by the prevailing currents a second island came into view. This was the main Auckland Island, clearly recognisable by its sheer cliff face that now loomed menacingly towards them. To those on board it was clear that the vessel was about to strike.

It was now that the lack of anything more than a moderate breeze was to prove something of an advantage. Instead of being dashed against this solid wall of rock the *General Grant* was only bumped and jarred. Where fierce winds or uncompromising breakers might have dashed the hull into matchwood, the gentle but persistent current claimed only her yardarms and protruding jibboom.

But the *General Grant* was not to be saved. The current that had brought her to the island had yet one more surprise in store. Continuing to control the vessel's course, it drove her along the island for about 800 yards before eventually forcing her inside a huge cavern that was about twice the length of the *General Grant*. Here, with her masts scraping across the domed roof, a sudden rock fall descended upon the ship. Although the upper decks were buried many of those on board were fortunate in surviving death or serious injury. Indeed, at that point, the worst appeared to be over. However, this was not to be.

The cavern, as a result of its position, was constantly subjected to a massive inrush of water. This, of course, had the effect of pushing the *General Grant* towards the end of the cave. As this happened, so more pressure was placed on the main and mizzen masts, eventually forcing one of them through the previously undamaged hull. As water began to gush into the vessel and with the clipper showing every sign of sinking, a mad panic ensued. Some simply threw themselves overboard and were drowned, while others desperately clambered into the three boats carried by the *General Grant*. The majority, some 40 passengers and crew, took to the long boat.

A combination of inexperience and sheer desperation probably accounts for the event that followed. As that crowded long boat began to edge out of the cave it was caught by the breakers and the back wash from the cliffs. Already low down in the water, the boat now began to heel, taking on board increasing quantities of water. Despite the efforts of those on board to bail her out, the long boat gradually sank, taking with her all but three of her passengers.

Those who had managed to get on board the other two boats were more fortunate. Between them they carried a total of 14 (including the survivors from the long boat) and as a result were not so weighted down. For this reason they managed to clear the danger area around the cliff face, eventually reaching calmer waters. Here a brief discussion ensued and it was decided that they should row for Disappointment Island. This was a fairly logical decision, it being impossible to beach the boats under the overhanging cliff face that ran along the side of the island on which they had been wrecked.

Because of the wind and current it took a good many hours to cover the seven miles that separated them from the smaller island, but eventually they reached it. Here, despite the island's off-putting name, they were able to find both shelter and drinking water, while a few albatrosses were trapped and used to supplement their own meagre food supplies. Events had overtaken them so rapidly that they had only been able to bring with them a few tins of soup and boiled meat.

The survivor's sojourn on Disappointment Island was to be short-lived. Their real intention was to reach the far side of Auckland where, so it was believed, a depot of provisions had been established for those unfortunate enough to be shipwrecked on the island. In recent years there had been two earlier vessels grounding there and it was believed that the supplies from one of them had been deliberately left behind, following an earlier rescue from the island. Unfortunately it was to prove a rather forlorn hope. Certainly, the survivors from the *General Grant* were able to return to the main Auckland Island, bringing the two boats into a bay on the far side of this island. However, as no deposited food supplies were to be discovered, the small group had then to fend for themselves. Relying entirely upon the natural resources of the island, combined with the experience and know-how of the remaining gold diggers, the 14 survivors embarked on a desperate hand-to-mouth period of existence. Surviving only on mussels, birds eggs, seal and albatross meat, they were to remain stranded on the Auckland Islands for about 18 months.

It was not until January 1868 that this group, by now reduced to 10, (one had died from illness and three attempted to sail to New Zealand), was eventually rescued. In that month, the *Amherst*, a brig engaged in the whaling trade, happened to pass close to the island and caught sight of the encampment. At the time the master of the whaler, Captain Glenroy, had no idea of the *General Grant*'s disappearance, no search having been mounted in this particular area of the ocean. As for the feelings of those few survivors upon boarding the *Amherst*, these are best summed up by one of the survivors when he declared: 'On nearing her a line was thrown to us, and we were taken on board. Words cannot express our feelings of joy for such a deliverance from hardship and privation during a period of eighteen months.'

So far in this account of the wreck of the *General Grant*, nothing has been said of the 'Flying Dutchman'. Admittedly, the nature of the wreck and the amazing hardships endured by the survivors is, in itself, an interesting story. But, overall, it would appear to have little to do with the subject matter of this chapter. Or does it?

According to at least one writer, the *General Grant* may have been lured to her watery grave by Vanderdecken himself. It seems that as the *General Grant* entered into those unfavourable currents that pushed her far south of her intended track she was joined by another vessel. Short and squat, she was more like a ship of old than the tall magnificent beauties that were normally to be found heading for Cape Horn.

Even more unusual however, was her ability to defy the prevailing winds. While the *General Grant* was having difficulty in beating to windward, the other ship appeared to command the winds. On several occasions she passed the *General Grant*, only to appear further to the west from where she would once again overhaul the labouring clipper. It was an uncanny experience that would have sent a shiver down the spines of any of those who dared watch the antics of this strange vessel.

It would not have been long before those on board the *General Grant* began drawing their own conclusions as to what this ship might be. For the superstitious there appeared to be only one possibility: this ancient ship must be nothing less than the accursed 'Flying Dutchman'. However, a closer examination of events leading up to the loss of the *General Grant* tends to throw a shadow of doubt over such a vessel having been seen. To begin with, none of the contemporary newspaper accounts relating to the *General Grant* make mention of such a vessel. Most of the 10 survivors, upon being landed in New Zealand, were interviewed, and extremely detailed accounts of their adventure were sent on to many of the world's newspapers. Surely, something as sensational as their being accompanied by the 'Flying Dutchman' would have deserved a few column inches in at least some of these newspapers. Despite the fact that I checked a number of them I could find no suggestion of a mystery ship having been sighted.

More important, however, is that no reference is made to the 'Flying Dutchman' story in a recently published and highly detailed account of the *General Grant*. Written by

Keith Eunson, and entitled *The Wreck of the General Grant*, the author has gone to a considerable amount of effort in uncovering every piece of information concerning the fatal voyage and subsequent loss of life as a result of the *General Grant* having entered that strange cave. Throughout the 164 pages of the book Eunson makes not one single reference to the 'Flying Dutchman'. Is it possible that a writer, in attempting to uncover every piece of background detail, would miss something as important as the *General Grant* being lured to her fate by the 'Flying Dutchman'?

Of further interest, is that Raymond Lamont-Brown, the writer who links both Vanderdecken and the *General Grant* goes on to add a few more details. He notes, correctly, that some of the survivors from the *General Grant* were to return to the Auckland Islands some months after the rescue. Their intention was that of removing some of the cargo from the splintered decks of the now submerged clipper.

Two of these survivors, according to Lamont-Brown, actually entered the fateful cavern while their steam tug remained anchored further out. As they seemingly disappeared into the cliff face, the 'Flying Dutchman' re-enters the story. Bearing down upon the single tug, those on board thought it was their lives she was after. But with collision all but inevitable this ancient sailing ship apparently veered to one side.

If this account is correct, and again there are reasons for doubting it, then the curse of the 'Flying Dutchman' must have been on those who had entered the cavern. None were to return. Those on board the tug were never to learn of their fate. They had simply disappeared, victims of the curse that had been placed upon Vanderdecken.

That this story should be doubted relates to the number of factual errors that, when corrected, make the sighting of the 'Flying Dutchman' quite impossible. The expedition referred to was probably one that took place during the year 1870. It did not, however, involve two survivors, but only one; David

Ashworth. Approaching the Auckland Islands in a 48-ton topsail schooner, and not a steam tug as Lamont-Brown suggests, a base camp was established at the north end of Auckland Island. It was here that the majority of the crew remained while Ashworth, together with the schooner's captain, took the whaleboat to investigate the difficulties that would be involved in salvaging the *General Grant*. It is not known whether they reached the cave, nor whether they entered it. All that is known is that the whale boat failed to return. Both men presumably drowned at sea. As for the sighting of the 'Flying Dutchman', again this appears to be pure fiction. If nothing else, the schooner, which carried the name *Daphne*, was most certainly not anchored off the cave during the period in which the two men disappeared.

Leaving aside these undoubtedly fabricated accounts of the 'Flying Dutchman', it is nevertheless a fact that a number of supposed sightings are extremely difficult to reject. Some, of course, have probably been exaggerated, but among those who claim to have seen the 'Flying Dutchman', and already recorded in this chapter, are a number of reliable seamen. After all, their numbers do include a future king of Great Britain, several German U-boat commanders and a sprinkling of Royal Navy officers. Surely, none of these individuals have anything to gain from a totally fabricated story?

It almost suggests that there might be a real 'Flying Dutchman' somewhere out there in the world's oceans!

The American clipper *General Grant* overshadowed by the tall unforgiving cliffs of the Auckland Islands. Was she lured by the 'Flying Dutchman'?

HMS *Eurydice* on the eve of her final voyage. Following her tragic loss many have reported seeing her spectre off the Isle of Wight. Below, the wreck of the *Eurydice* is towed into Portsmouth Harbour.

11

The Ghost of *Eurydice*

There is one ship, over all others, that truly deserves to be included in any account of phantoms on the high seas. She is HMS *Eurydice*, a British navy sail training ship wrecked off Dunnose Point, Isle of Wight, in March 1878. Since the time of her sudden and unexpected demise she has frequently been linked with hauntings and premonitions. In every way she demands a starring role in a book that touches upon aspects of the supernatural maritime world.

Eurydice began life in 1843 as a two decked full rigged sailing frigate. In appearance she was not outwardly different from generations of earlier vessels that had valiantly served the Royal Navy in countless actions around the world. In particular, *Eurydice* was recognised as possessing exceptional sea keeping qualities, a fact that helped her outlive many of her contemporaries. Surviving into the age of steam and iron, she was converted into a sea going training ship in 1877, involving a number of internal alterations. *Eurydice* was stripped of all but four of her twenty-four guns and provided with a number of additional cabins and stores.

Following her conversion *Eurydice* was placed under the command of Captain the Hon. Marcus Augustus Hare RN. He was an experienced and competent officer who had served on board a great number of sea going ships prior to this appointment. Of particular value for the task in hand was his recent command of another sail training ship. This was HMS *St Vincent*, a former first rate which had then been moored in Portsmouth Harbour. Although Captain Hare never took *St*

Vincent to sea it did give him the necessary practical experience in the training of recruits. Throughout his time on board *St Vincent* Captain Hare proved a popular officer and one who easily gained the confidence and respect of those who served under him.

After her refit *Eurydice* left Portsmouth for the West Indies on 13 November 1877. It was to be her first and only cruise as a training ship. On board were some 300 crew, the majority of whom were the young ordinary seamen under training. In addition to the officers and petty officers there was also a leavening of more experienced seamen on board. Over the next few months, *Eurydice* was based in the Caribbean, undergoing joint manouevres with two other training ships, the brigs *Martin* and *Liberty*. Both of these vessels returned to England before *Eurydice*.

That *Eurydice* did not accompany the two brigs was the result of a last minute change of plan. Captain Hare was ordered to take her to Bermuda where he was to embark 35 passengers. For the most part these were Army officers returning home upon the expiry of their service abroad, but the passengers also included several court martialled naval ratings who were being sent home for punishment. Finally, on March 6th *Eurydice* left Bermuda.

For the most part the cruise home was uneventful. Favourable winds helped speed her along and the vessel entered the English Channel on the morning of March 24th. Captain Hare now chose a course that would allow his ship to pass along the south side of the Isle of Wight before rounding the island to enter Portsmouth. The *Eurydice* was reported approaching Dunnose Head in the south-east of the island at 3.30 that same afternoon. According to the coastguard at nearby Bonchurch *Eurydice* was 'moving fast under all sail, studding on fore and main, bonnets and skyscrapers'. In other words, she had virtually every sail hoisted. Captain Hare was, apparently, determined to reach Portsmouth before nightfall.

It being Sunday, the customary naval convention of using

the afternoon for 'make and mend' had been duly allowed. Some, of course, may have been doing exactly this, undertaking essential repairs on their much frayed working clothes. The majority however, were simply relaxing. Starboard watch, consisting of 150 seamen, was down below, some of them asleep, others letter writing or reading. To ensure that this rather packed area was properly ventilated all but four of the gun ports had been left open.

On deck, and due to remain there until eight bells of the Afternoon Watch (4pm) had been sounded, were an equal number of seamen who made up port watch, but most of these too had only limited duties. Those not directly involved in steering or look-out or required for trimming sails took advantage of the clear and sunny weather to gaze wistfully at the passing cliffs, no doubt glad to be home again.

To those on shore the beautiful sight of a three masted sailing ship ploughing rapidly through the waters around the island attracted a good deal of attention. Among those who saw her were several old salts who were reminded of their own days aboard similar ships. Another group who witnessed *Eurydice*'s progress was a small party of ramblers who were following the cliff top path that led to Sandown. Despite near freezing temperatures and a steadily rising wind they gave the vessel a few moments of their time. Attracted by her immaculate snow white sails and jet black hull, they considered her a sight 'par excellence'.

Although self-confessed landsmen this group of walkers was not convinced as to her complete safety. Battered as they were by near storm force winds, they believed her to be carrying too much sail. Indeed, they observed several other ships in the act of shortening their sails, the crew of these vessels seemingly aware of an ominously black storm cloud approaching from the north-west. One of the group, signing himself 'Viator', later wrote a letter to *The Times* referring to the *Eurydice* and went so far as to call it questionable seamanship. However, such a judgement may have been somewhat misplaced given the precise circumstances. As HMS *Eurydice* passed within view of the walkers she found herself in temporarily sheltered waters. Indeed, those on board were completely oblivious to the steadily rising wind. The cliff face, along which she was passing, some 500 ft in height, acted as a perfect wind break. Despite the crowded canvas that hung from every spar, those on board *Eurydice* were aware of only a moderate breeze. As for the impending storm, the warning clouds, approaching from the north-west, were completely obscured.

Another who appears to have seen *Eurydice* as she passed along those south facing cliffs of the Isle of Wight was a retired diplomat Sir John MacNeill. Unlike the ramblers, he was nowhere near Dunnose Point and the impending tragedy. Instead, he was safely ensconced in the warmth of his apartment at Windsor, 65 miles away as the crow flies, sharing tea with his cousin, the Right Reverend Dr Boyd Carpenter, Bishop of Ripon, and Sir John Cowell. Gazing out of the window he was suddenly heard to exclaim, 'Good Heavens! Why don't they close the port holes and reef the topsails!'

A bemused Cowell found it difficult to understand what his friend meant by this outburst. MacNeill himself was unable to enlighten him. All that he could say was that he had seen a ship coming up the Channel under full sail and with her port holes open. Above the vessel was a thick black storm cloud. To MacNeill's mind the vessel appeared to be doomed.

On board *Eurydice*, the Officer of the Watch noticed the barometer was beginning to fall in a rather alarming fashion. However, nobody considered this to be a serious problem. The storm cloud was still hidden while *Eurydice*, herself, was still being pushed along by nothing more than a moderate breeze. The ship's captain was, however, informed of the new barometer reading. At about the same moment that Captain Hare appeared on deck *Eurydice* entered less protected waters as she crossed Sandown Bay. As she left the lee of the high cliffs her sails began to billow under an increased pressure of wind. It was time to reef. Now for the first time those on board saw the black cloud heading over the land directly for them. This is what the falling barometer had portended. Already a thick curtain of snow was blanking out part of the shore line.

Immediately Captain Hare directed the port watch to take in the lower studding sails hoisted earlier in the afternoon to catch the ligher winds that had then predominated. But even when these were taken in it was clear that the ship was far from secure. The royals and other light weather sails would also have to be furled.

'Watch, in upper sails', was the urgent instruction now given to the young seamen as the first blast of a vicious snow storm hit the ship. Within a few minutes a vast cloud had hidden the sun, casting the ship into semi-darkness. A gale force wind and swirling thick snow now made movement on board the vessel extremely treacherous. Fearing that the upper masts might snap at any moment Captain Hare felt forced to recall the duty watch, ordering the men to return immediately to the comparative safety of the deck.

Already the pressure of wind on the canvas was forcing the ship to heel dangerously to starboard. Water was pouring over the upper deck and through the gaping holes of the open ports. Unable to shorten sail and aware of how close the ship was to sinking, Captain Hare turned his attention to those at the wheel. 'Luff and shake it out of her', he yelled to the quartermaster, his voice only just audible over the roar of gale. His intention was to bring *Eurydice* closer to the wind. Unfortunately, with her bows also partly under water, the action of the helmsman merely had the effect of driving her deeper. Even more water began to enter through the forward ports.

Below deck pandemonium broke out. As more and more water began to pour in through the open ports, members of starboard watch rushed to the companionway. Only a few reached the top of the ladder. With *Eurydice* heeling at such an extreme angle it was only a few seconds before masses of gushing freezing water cascaded over the top of the ship and along all of the available escape routes. So violent was this new in-rush of water that it ripped out the companionway ladders, effectively trapping the remainder of starboard watch.

Aware that his ship was now lost, Hare was heard to mutter, 'it is of no avail'. Shortly after, he gave the crew their final instructions, 'Every man for himself.' But even this came too late. *Eurydice* was already in her death throes and had started to capsize.

In those fatal minutes over 300 men were drowned. Some managed to throw themselves overboard, but the vast majority were sucked or dragged down with the ship. Those who were able to jump into the sea were, for the most part, only prolonging their lives for a few extra minutes. It had been an exceptionally cold winter and the waters of the English Channel were close to freezing. With rescue ships unable to reach these survivors for over an hour, the majority perished.

In fact there were only two survivors from the entire ship's complement: Ordinary Seaman Sidney Fletcher and Able Seaman Benjamin Cuddiford. Both were picked up by the schooner *Emma*. Lying further out to sea than *Eurydice*, the *Emma* had been one of those vessels that walkers along the cliff top had seen shortening her sails. In fact the *Emma*, too, had been proceeding under full sail but because of her more favourable position, the impending storm had been seen. The *Emma*'s master, Captain Langworthy Jenkins, had ordered his crew to take in the mainsail, flying jib, staysails and top sails, leaving only the jib. For this reason the *Emma* was able to ride out the storm which Jenkins described as a sudden snow squall that lasted no more than thirty minutes.

Prior to the storm it appears that those on board the *Emma* had not seen *Eurydice*. However, once the snow had cleared they saw a great deal of wreckage floating around them and heard a man shouting. Setting sail and then steering in the direction of the voice they were able to pick up the only two survivors from the disaster.

Aware that *Eurydice* was due to arrive at Portsmouth sometime that Sunday afternoon, those with sons, husbands, brothers and sweethearts began to gather outside the dock-yard gate. In one small Gosport home the recently married Eleanor Lake looked forward to the return of her brother, David Thomas Bennett. They had not seen each other for over four months and they had much to share in the way of news. As always, David would have a small present for his sister, allowing her to come one step closer in the sharing of her much travelled brother's latest adventure. At around 3.50pm she suddenly felt pangs of intense anxiety. As she later confided to her husband and other members of the family, she knew then and there that something awful had happened.

Trying to dismiss these fears, her attention was drawn to the familiar sound of David's footsteps on the garden path. He was home at last! Overwhelmed with relief she rushed to the door, fully expecting to see his happy beaming face. But as she threw the door open all her hopes were to be dashed. There was no one there. Search as she might, she could find no one in the garden or anyone else nearby. It was at that moment that she became finally convinced that her brother, an Able Seaman on the *Eurydice*, had somehow died. It was only on the following day that she learnt of the awful tragedy which had taken not only her brother's life, but that of so many of his comrades.

It is possible that other souls from *Eurydice* also returned to their loved ones on the hour of their death. In doing so it must be assumed that their task was to ease the burden of grief. It was to be many months before *Eurydice* was raised, by which time many of the bodies were unrecognisable. Rather than allow their families to believe that they might hope that they were alive, their spirits were determined to forewarn and ease the period of anguish.

Even stranger than a returning ghost from among those who served on board the *Eurydice* was the ghost of the ship herself! Although her battered and useless hull was eventually salvaged and later broken up, it does appear that she might still haunt those treacherous waters south of Dunnose Point. Within a year or two of the disaster local fishermen began to report a number of strange happenings. Some claimed they had seen a full rigged sailing ship moving at considerable speed. As it approached them, it would simply disappear. Various rational explanations have been put forward to explain this particular phenomenon. Some have suggested that it results from a trick of the light, while others have put it down to reflections caused by sea mist. But most of the local fishermen remained convinced that it was the ghost of HMS *Eurydice* that had been witnessed.

The best authenticated account of the apparition of a three masted sailing ship comes from the pen of a hard headed naval officer, Commander F. Lipscombe. He claims that during the 1930s, while in command of a submarine, he nearly collided with a sailing man o' war off the Isle of Wight. Deciding to investigate the incident, he subsequently visited the island and interviewed a number of local inhabitants. He was given one, and only one, explanation – it was the wraith of the tragic *Eurydice*.

With her sails still set *Eurydice* comes under the influence of a sudden and unexpected squall. Was it this sight which was inexplicably witnessed by Sir John MacNeill? Below, The Prince of Wales (later King Edward VII) visiting the *Eurydice* while salvage operations were in progress. In excess of 300 died as a result of her capsizing. The spirit of at least one of these victims is thought to have returned to shore.

12

Smuggling Haunts

The Sicilian 'mafioso' has a reputation for violence, but this pales into insignificance when compared with the campaigns of terror frequently mounted by the old time smuggling fraternities that once ringed the British Isles. Desperate to ensure the silence of all who knew of their activities, these gangs were invariably associated with extreme acts of violence.

All too often they were prepared to murder, torture and maim any who were thought likely to inform. As a result innocent local villagers who may accidentally have seen or heard too much went in constant fear of their lives. If they were considered untrustworthy, then members of the fraternity would carry out a midnight visit that always ended in bloodshed. For the unfortunate villager there was no means of appeal. It was, quite simply, the law of the jungle.

Of course, such a picture clashes with the normally romantic image of the smuggler that has grown up over the years. As a result of numerous films and novels the 18th century smuggler has acquired a sympathetic following. Often, such individuals are seen as mere tax evaders whose single aim was to bring a small amount of wealth and prosperity to areas that had previously seen only poverty and hunger. In some cases this might have been true. Certainly there were a number of villages where the occasional 'run' was freely supported by the entire community.

Within such an area, a locally owned fishing boat would unaccountably disappear for a few days, its destination either the Channel Islands or the nearest mainland European port. On its return the boat would be met by a group of farm labourers who would act as tub carriers. They would quickly unload the boat, transferring its illicit cargo of spirits or tea to a suitable hiding place. Sometimes, as in the best of smuggling fiction, the place of concealment was either the local manor house or parish church, with the squire or parson taking a small share of those much sought after luxury items.

However, this rather 'amateur' approach to smuggling was somewhat overshadowed by the likes of the Hawkhurst and Aldington gangs. Between them, these particular gangs controlled huge areas of coastline and had the ability to call upon several hundred sympathisers to support the numerous 'runs' that were made each and every month. Many of those who took a share in the profits were nothing more than paid thugs, their role being that of frightening the local community into silence.

To combat such smuggling activities the British government established a preventive force run by HM Customs and Excise. In a number of the larger coastal towns, Customs Houses were established, with several appointed officers responsible for the collection of excise duties on goods either entering or leaving the country. When necessary the senior officer of the Customs House, known as the Collector, could call upon the services of an armed force of soldiers to help in the apprehension of any person or group suspected of involvement in smuggling activities.

However, most of the large smuggling fraternities chose to operate in areas distant from the collection ports. In fact, the larger and more sophisticated gangs tended to be found in more isolated areas where the presence of any customs officer could be easily monitored. To infiltrate these areas, the preventive force also had at its disposal a group of individuals known as Riding Officers. Their duties were to patrol the more isolated parts of the kingdom, with each officer responsible for an area of coastline that might range in length from four to ten miles. As can be easily imagined, riding officers had a fairly perilous existence, especially if they took their job seriously.

Imagine, if you will, the lonely riding officer. His main duty was patrolling a long stretch of coast that might include a range of towering cliffs or a huge stretch of eerie marshland. As he rode this nightly patrol (for smugglers would rarely 'run' a cargo during daylight hours) he would be in constant fear of attack. Every shadow, every sound or sudden movement might represent the first sign of a merciless band of cut throats.

Of course, if our riding officer did come upon a small vessel unloading a precious cargo (or a suspicious group of farm labourers clustered around a small inlet), he could always call upon the services of a local military detachment – if he had the time. But as the nearest barracks might be more than 20 miles away this was most likely an impossibility. Instead, a riding officer in this situation could aim to do little more than remain concealed, hoping to recognise one or two familiar faces. In the morning, having called on some military help, it might just be possible to make a few arrests – but even then the charge might not stick. Any named individual would almost certainly have an unbreakable alibi, while the local magistrate, before whom he might have to appear, could even be a supporter of that same smuggling gang. As a result, even an identified smuggler rarely had anything to fear.

As an alternative to a nocturnal patrol, some riding officers concentrated on gathering information. For such purposes they would often base themselves in a local ale house, their ears ever open for the occasional piece of gossip. By this means, it might be possible to discover a vital clue that would lead to the discovery of a hidden tunnel or some new hiding place that contained a few dozen bags of tea or a tub of Geneva.

The strength of the smuggler and the weakness of the riding officer is ably demonstrated by the numerous minute books and items of correspondence still to be found in the archives of the Customs and Excise offices in London. Of particular interest is a whole series of letter books that once belonged to John Collier, Surveyor-General of Riding Officers for the counties of Kent and Sussex. Written during the middle years of the 18th century, they tell of many failed attempts to arrest and convict members of the smuggling fraternity. Take this letter which was written to Collier during the year 1734 and which refers to the strength of the smuggling gangs that were then operating from Lydd, a small town close to the centre of the Romney Marshes: 'Here they pass to and from the seaside 40 or 50 in a gang in the day time, loaded with tea, brandy and dry goods; that above 200 smugglers mounted were seen one night upon the sea beach there, waiting for the loading of six boats, and above 100 were seen to go off, all loaded with goods.'

The commissioners in London accepted this statement and a force of 19 dragoons was sent to the Romney Marsh area. This force was to have very little influence on the situation, other than to encourage the smugglers to become even more heavily armed.

Another example of this state affairs in the Romney Marsh area can be seen in a letter written to Collier by Mr Clare, the Customs Supervisor for Hythe: 'I came to Romney about 6pm and went to the Rose and Crown . . . to my surprise the stables were filled with smugglers' horses, so that my mare was carried to a private stable. I went to my chambers – sent for the Romney officers, who came with their books, which I examined and signed. We lamented our condition, that such quantities of goods must be suffered to be run before our faces, and we not able to take or prevent any of it.'

The following day, Clare goes on to record, about 18 smugglers took over the whole town. They were well armed with pistols, brass 'ffusees' and various other weapons. They commandeered the *Dolphin* and *Rose and Crown* for breakfast before leaving the town in an ostentatious manner.

One riding officer in the Romney area tried to carry out his job with every degree of diligence, only to find himself in great difficulty. This was Mr Darby of Scotney. In a letter to Collier, Clare reported: 'The smugglers have got to such height of impudence at Lydd, that they have drove Mr Darby and his wife and family from their habitation, threatening to murder him if they can catch him . . . All officers in my district are afraid to go out of their houses.'

All Kent was infested with gangs of smugglers. In October 1742 Daniel Barker, Customs House Officer, wrote to Collier stating that Tonbridge was saturated with large gangs who freely rode through the town. In March 1746 Mr Ketcherell, Customs Officer at Canterbury, reported that a gang of 150 smugglers landed their cargo between Reculver and Birchington. Later about 63 of them rode brazenly through Whitstable and Faversham.

The fact that these examples of the difficulties that confronted customs men are all drawn from the Kent and Romney Marsh area is no mere coincidence. For over 500 years this one county of England was the centre of operations for some of the most highly organised and ruthless of the 'free traders' (as the smugglers usually called themselves). Beginning in the 14th century with the illicit export of wool, they slowly turned their attentions to the import trade, taking advantage of excessively high taxes that had been placed upon tea, spirits and a variety of other luxury goods.

With such a long history of evading taxes, coupled with the willingness of such gangs to slaughter all those who might oppose them, it is hardly surprising that this same area should also be littered with a huge variety of ghost stories. For the most part they have their origins in the clashes that took place between the smuggler and the forces of law and order.

A particularly gruesome story of a ghost from the heyday of smuggling comes, not surprisingly, from the Romney Marshes. It concerns a nameless member of one of the numerous gangs. For reasons of greed, so it must be supposed,

this foolish individual chose to make himself rich by outwardly supporting the nocturnal activities of the smugglers,
while reporting all that he knew to one of the local riding
officers. In this way, he gave himself two sources of income,
for not only did the smuggling gangs pay handsomely for the
help they were given, but the government was also generous
in the allocation of rewards to those who were prepared to
inform.

In time of course the ever alert 'free traders' learnt of this
traitor in their midst. A number of eager volunteers stepped
forward for the purpose of taking revenge on the traitor who
was soon fighting for his life. To deter others by making a
widely known example of him it was decided to cut his body
into several pieces and scatter them around the marshes. This
has led to a rather fanciful story in which it is said that on dark,
moonless nights, this brave but foolish man still wanders the
marsh. His object is to discover the missing parts of his body,
for only then will he be able to rest in peace.

In Staplehurst, a Kent village that stands to the north of the
Romney Marshes, it is said that the ghost of George Beesley
may occasionally be seen. He was a member of the infamous
Hawkhurst gang, a fraternity of smugglers who dominated
much of the south coast of England during the early part of
the eighteenth century. So sophisticated an organisation did
this gang once possess, that they could literally collect
together, within an hour, over 500 armed men. In this situation, what hope was there for the poor lonely riding officer?

Frequently the fast cutters used by the Hawkhurst gang
could be seen making rapid passage to one of the northern
ports of France or to the Channel Islands. After a few days,
during which time several hundred 'pipes', (100 gallon casks),
of Geneva might have been loaded on board, together with a
consignment of tea or tobacco, this same vessel would begin
her return passage. This time her destination would be one of
the secluded coves of Kent, Sussex or Hampshire.

Rarely were these 'runs' interfered with, the smuggled

cargo usually being sold for a huge profit on the open market. The frequency of such 'runs' and the potential for making large sums of money, meant that a good many of the Hawkhurst gang soon became rich and respected members of the local community. One former leader of the gang, a certain Arthur Gray, was even in a position to construct a lavish mansion, known as 'Gray's Folly', on land just west of the village of Hawkhurst.

During a period of approximately 20 years' activity, the Hawkhurst gang were responsible for a number of violent acts that included the murder of several preventive officers and a daring punitive attack upon an entire village community which had ceased co-operating with the gang. Perhaps the act for which the gang gained greatest notoriety resulted from an armed attack upon the Customs House at Poole in Dorset, carried out in October 1747. In this particular building, so it might be supposed, any goods confiscated by the preventive force might well have been considered secure. But this was far from being the situation.

The Hawkhurst gang, having recently had a large consignment of tea amounting in value to about £500 seized by the Customs decided that such a large investment should not be lost without a fight. Following a meeting in Charlton Forest some 30 of them marched on Poole, while a similar number took control of the roads leading into the town. Ignoring the presence of an armed sloop, whose guns were actually ranged upon the Customs House, they forced open one of the doors to the building and simply removed all that they considered rightfully to be their property.

As for George Beesley, he may or may not have been present during this attack upon the Customs House. But, in his own right, he had become a man that the authorities greatly wished to have under lock and key. Aware that he was normally to be found in a small farmhouse just outside the village of Staplehurst, a troop of dragoons was sent to the village to arrest him. As the soldiers battered their way through the entrance door, Beesley attempted to make his escape. Having given previous thought to the matter, it was his intention to climb the chimney and then lower himself from the roof and into the yard immediately beyond. However, things did not work quite as he had planned. Perhaps the door gave too quickly, or he was not as sprightly as he might have been. Either way, before he could reach the inglenook, the door had given and he was caught in the act of escaping. Not prepared to see their quarry disappear, one of the dragoons fired and George Beesley fell to the ground.

On winter nights, so a local village tradition tells us, George Beesley re-enacts those last desperate seconds of his life. Suddenly, in this same farmhouse, and from out of nowhere, a translucent figure is to be seen running towards the large inglenook fire place. Of course, the figure never quite reaches its destination, for it suddenly disappears in the middle of the room!

A later group of smugglers to be found on the Romney Marshes was the Aldington gang known, for a not particularly obvious reason, as 'The Blues'. Their heyday was the period immediately after the Napoleonic Wars and they too could quickly muster huge numbers of armed thugs to support any of their more profitable ventures.

Unlike the Hawkhurst gang, 'The Blues' were operating during a period in which the cards were finally being stacked against the smuggler. The government had, at last, decided to put an end to this reign of terror that hovered over Britain's southern coastline. To this end, the Royal Navy was ordered to carry out regular land and sea patrols, with two large warships anchored in strategic locations. As a result, smuggling gangs operating during this period had to be better organised and more heavily armed than any of their predecessors.

The Aldington gang, in particular, tended to operate with a military like precision. Having decided when and where a 'run' was to be made, the beach to be used for unloading the

The Walnut Tree. A Kentish village pub haunted by the ghosts of two former smugglers.

vessel was first surrounded by armed look-outs. Once the cargo had been removed from the boats the tub carriers would quickly transfer it to a local farm house, the members of the armed cordon going on to scour the local countryside to make sure that none of these activities had been observed. On the few occasions when a naval patrol did stumble upon an unloading vessel a regular armed fight would result. While other, smaller gangs might be forced to surrender, the Aldington gang was frequently better armed and able to resist arrest or the capture of their illicit cargo.

It is likely that a number of stories of haunted beaches along the Kent and Sussex coastline have their origins in these many fights that took place between the Royal Navy and armed groups of smugglers. However, for the Aldington gang, their most celebrated ghost is that of George Ransley, leader of 'The Blues' from the year 1821 onwards. Ransley was another of those individuals who greatly prospered from 'free trading'. Like Arthur Gray of the Hawkhurst gang he also put his money into property, purchasing the *Bourne Tap*, an ale house that once stood in the village of Aldington.

However, the gang's real headquarters was another ale-house, *The Walnut Tree*. It is this particular building, still known by that name, which houses the ghost of the former leader of 'The Blues'. It was not as a result of Ransley meeting his fate here, but rather his long term connections with the building, for Ransley is buried in Tasmania where he was transported after his eventual arrest for smuggling. One assumes, therefore, that the spirit, having become free of Ransley's body, made its own return to a place for which he had probably held deep affection.

Incredibly there is a second smuggler's ghost with an attachment to *The Walnut Tree*. This one was also a member of the Aldington gang, though this time not a leader, but an ordinary rank and file member who was killed during a violent quarrel. In an attempt to conceal the crime the body was placed in a conveniently located water barrel. Possibly this phantom continues to haunt *The Walnut Tree* in the hope that it might one day revenge itself on the man who struck the mortal blow.

Other old Kentish smuggling haunts exist on the Isle of Thanet, an area that includes the modern seaside towns of Margate, Ramsgate and Broadstairs. Here, so tradition will have us believe, Riding Officer Anthony Gill and the smuggler he was chasing both lost their lives when they fell into a chalk pit towards the beginning of the 18th century. It is frequently stated that both smuggler and riding officer are seen to re-enact this final struggle.

So enduring did this story become that Thomas Ingoldsby, creator of *The Ingoldsby Legends* wrote a poem, *Smuggler's Leap* to commemorate the event. The following verses pick up the tale where the smuggler, mounted on a particularly fast steed, attempts to jump the quarry, with Gill in hot pursuit:

> To stand on that fearful verge, and peep
> Down the rugged sides so dreadfully steep,
> Where the chalk-hole yawns full sixty feet deep,
> O'er which that steed took that desperate leap!
> It was so dark then under the trees,
> No horse in the world could tell chalk from cheese –
> Down they went – o'er that terrible fall, –
> Horses, Exciseman, Smuggler, and all!!
>
> Below were found Next day on the ground
> By an elderly gentleman walking his round,
> (I wouldn't have seen such a sight for a pound,)
> All smash'd and dash'd, three mangled corpses,
> Two of them human – the third was a horse's –
> That good dapple grey, and Exciseman Gill
> Yet grasping the collar of Smuggler Bill!

Outside the county of Kent the smuggling lairs of Britain stretched from Yorkshire in the north-east to Cornwall in the south-west and all of them have their own ghost stories. A number of these hauntings result from desperate struggles

that took place between smugglers and excise men or between one smuggling gang and another. Take for example the
phantom that walks the village of Happisburgh in Norfolk.
Both legless and virtually decapitated, for the head is held by
a mere sinew, it glides along the main road before entering
this isolated coastal village.

Although not definitely confirmed to be a ghost of a smuggler, its first sighting in 1765 more or less coincides with a
series of desperate struggles then taking place between different gangs of smugglers. All accounts of sightings of this apparition have the legless body disappearing at a point known as
Well Corner, where there was indeed a well. So the well itself
was eventually searched and at the bottom were discovered
the skeletal remains of a body that was partially bereft of its
head. In addition, the leg bones were found to have been
wrapped in an accompanying canvas bag. Signs, indeed, of a
bloody murder having been committed!

Two smuggling haunts in the West Country are Morvah in
Cornwall and Shepton Mallet in Somerset. At Morvah, a
north facing fishing and former smuggling village approximately nine miles south-west of St Ives, a ghostly crew of
smugglers supposedly make an appearance on the once des-
olate beach. According to those who claim to have seen this
particular apparition, each of the smugglers is weighed down
by a tub of brandy. Even more interesting is that this same
scene also includes a number of spectral horses. One assumes
that they have been brought to the site in order to speed this
illicit cargo on its way.

As for Shepton Mallet, though far from the sea it became a
trading centre for illicit goods and has the apparition of a
hanged smuggler. It seems that on certain dark nights, at a
point just a mile south of the town, a gibbet and errant
smuggler suddenly appear before the eyes of unsuspecting
travellers.

To conclude this brief summary of smuggling haunts, it is
impossible to ignore a particularly remarkable event that

sometimes takes place on the coast at Whitby in Yorkshire. Here, accompanied by loud bangs and hideous screams, an old time clash between a group of smugglers and excisemen is re-enacted. Despite the ear splitting noises that result from this fracas, not all in the area are able to witness the event. Apparently, it appears only to the most sensitive, others living nearby are seemingly oblivious to the mad struggle that is going on around them.

Before ending this particular chapter, it occurs to me that there is a point of significance in the nature of these various smuggling stories. All of them are drawn from the 18th and early 19th centuries – the romantic age of the smuggler. More recent smugglers, including those involved in the widespread movement of diamonds, drugs and pornography, never seem to re-appear in a spiritual form. Is it possible that a modern public distaste for these activities is somehow connected with a dearth of such stories? Maybe those who have witnessed the ghost of a smuggler, and who are frequently unaware or unmindful of their more violent deeds, do so because of some innate sympathy with the smugglers' motives. Why else have we yet to hear numerous tales of haunted airports and modern seaports? The modern currency smuggler or trader in pornography is just as committed to his cause, it is just that the damage that these activities create is far more to the forefront. For this reason, there is no romantic appeal in witnessing such a ghost. As a result, few, if any, have ever been seen.

But on the beaches around the British Isles, where brandy, gin and tea smugglers once dominated, matters are very different!

13

Into The Teeth Of Death

Lying approximately 12 miles off the New England coast-line can be found Block Island, known to its original native American settlers as the Isle of the Little God. For much of this century it has proved a popular vacation resort, its expansive sandy beaches ideal for surfing, sunbathing and general relaxation.

However, Block Island's real attraction is its apparent timelessness. Seemingly, it has never travelled further forward than the late nineteenth century. Admittedly a few motor vehicles are to be found on the island, while daringly cut and carefully fashioned swimsuits are very definitely of the present age. But in most other respects the island is an idyllic reflection of bygone times.

Life on Block Island is generally unhurried. The most common means of getting round is a bicycle, while not one of its twenty-odd miles of road carries a single traffic light. The island also lacks fast food chains, plush luxury hotels, casinos and golf courses. Instead Block Island offers several harbour-side restaurants that specialise in sea food, while for those who choose to stay overnight, there is a range of guest houses offering unsurpassed ocean views. Even the local Chamber of Commerce prefers to extol the virtues of the island's gently rolling hillsides, rambling stone fences and 'quaint architecture that is vintage Victorian'. Above all, so one of its published brochures goes on to declare, there is a refreshing sea breeze 'that blows from some point of the compass all Summer long.'

A pleasant, Block Island, summer-time beach. In winter months, with heavy seas pounding across the sands, a phantom light can be seen on the horizon. Below, New Shoreham life saving station, which has since been transferred to Mystic Seaport (Connecticut), once stood on Block Island. The islanders, who manned it frequently risked their lives to save those on board endangered ships and were not wreckers as suggested by the oft-told tale of the non-existent *Palatine*.

But in winter, of course, when the vacation set have returned to their bustling offices, fast cars and multi-laned highways, the island presents a very different face. It is then that those refreshing breezes become ferocious winds that are both troublesome and dangerous, turning surfing waves into giant rollers. These same winds have brought tragedy and hardship to sailors unfortunate enough to have been caught in those waters at such times.

It was a severe northerly wind that finally brought the fore and aft rigged *Princess Augusta* crashing on to the island during the final week of December 1738. Throughout the previous four months she had been painfully making her way across the Atlantic, her holds crammed with sick and frightened immigrants, each one hoping to start life anew in the promised lands around Philadelphia.

In the event, only a mere handful were ever to reach the American mainland. The vast majority died on board the *Princess Augusta*, most of them succumbing to a whole series of unidentified diseases that were collectively recorded as 'flux'. Others died when the ship crashed aground on Sandy Point, a dangerous spit of land that lies to the north of Block Island. Perhaps it was inevitable that those on board the *Princess Augusta*, in suffering such hardships, should give rise to one of America's most enduring ghost stories!

It had been during the summer of 1738 that the *Princess Augusta* began that lengthy and ultimately tragic voyage across the Atlantic. At the English port of Ramsgate, where the vessel was registered, a crew of 14 had been assembled. Amongst them were George Long and Andrew Brook, respectively her captain and first mate. Little is really known about either man, although it can be safely assumed, judging by his later behaviour, that Brook must already have had a reputation for unscrupulous behaviour and general dishonesty.

As for the *Princess Augusta*, she was very much a typical working ship of the period. With proud masts stretching towards the clouds above, she was a mass of canvas, rigging and spars that had a complexity which could only be untangled by those born to the sea. Of 220 tons and measuring slightly less than 100 ft in length she would appear, when judged by today's standards, to be small for an Atlantic crossing, but stout oak ships and stout experienced men could face anything.

To protect the vessel, for there was always the possibility at that date of being attacked by pirates, the *Princess Augusta* carried eight smooth bore canon that each fired a solid stone ball. They were positioned on the lower decks, four on each side. Her crew, some of them probably trained on board British naval ships, might well have been able to fire these guns at the rate of one shot every two minutes. Although this small number of guns did not compare with the 309 or more that might be carried by warships of that period, they were deemed sufficient to scare off any pirate or privateer.

However, in the event, these guns were to prove quite useless. The *Princess Augusta* was captured by pirates, but these loathsome individuals were already on board, taking the form of First Mate Andrew Brook and a few like-minded deck hands.

It was probably in July that the *Princess Augusta* left Ramsgate. On this occasion she headed in a north-easterly direction, to make her first call at the Dutch port of Rotterdam where she took on board a human cargo of 350 refugees. All were crammed into the 'tween decks space that only allowed each individual sufficient room for eating, sleeping and breathing.

The bulk of these ill-fated refugees were protestant dissidents from the German state of Palatine. Having suffered equally from foreign invasion and religious bigotry, many of their number had already gone to America. For the most part, those earlier settlers favoured the lands around Philadelphia, so explaining why those on board the *Princess Augusta* were making for the same area. In doing so, they also hoped to share the improved life style already witnessed by their co-religionists from the state of Palatine.

As they came on board the *Princess Augusta* it would not have gone unnoticed by the crew that these refugees brought with them a great quantity of wealth. To make the voyage many of them had been forced to sell their various landholdings, property and cherished possessions, representing a life time of labour. This had now been converted into vast amounts of gold coin, silver plate and rich jewels. It was all they possessed and was to be used for the purpose of re-establishing themselves in the 'New World'. Leaving Rotterdam, the *Princess Augusta* sailed into the English Channel, taking on fresh supplies of food and water at Cowes and Plymouth. Finally, in August, she set course for America.

Although the various groups of Palatines and other immigrants suffered greatly in these early trans-Atlantic voyages, those on board the *Princess Augusta* suffered particular hardships. Trapped in an overcrowded, ill-ventilated cargo space, many were initially struck down with sea sickness. The stench of vomit soon permeated the entire ship, with recovery of those who suffered greatly hampered by the infrequency with which those on board were allowed access to the upper deck. However, this was to prove the least of their worries, with a far more disastrous illness striking just a few weeks later.

As the fresh supplies taken on board in England became exhausted, it was necessary to break into a caché of stocks previously shipped at Rotterdam. While the stored pork and damp biscuits may have tasted foul, for it had been kept in far from ideal conditions, it was at least edible. The water, as was realised at a later stage, was not even up to this standard. Having been stored in dirty and mouldy wine casks, some of it had become seriously polluted.

Unaware of the danger they were in, passengers and crew drank heavily from the first of these casks. None of them took any notice of the tiny amounts of mould to be seen clinging to the damp wood. For a short time, the warm water partially slaked the thirst of those who had drunk. However, just a few hours later, the poison took effect. Over 300 were struck down by a burning fever. Some eventually recovered, but over 100 died. Amongst the latter were Captain Long and seven of the crew.

The ship was now in the hands of Andrew Brook. With only half the crew having survived the fever, he had his work cut out. In addition, matters were not made any easier by the weather. Over the next few weeks the *Princess Augusta* was caught by a number of terrible storms. Pushed further and further north, those on board doubtless felt that the voyage would never end.

For the cramped passengers their situation became even less palatable as a result of the actions of the former first mate towards them. Unlike his passengers Andrew Brook was no God-fearing zealot. Indeed, he seems to have taken an instant dislike to the humble Palatines with whom he shared the vessel. Instead of offering them sustenance and pity, he slammed the hatches down. From now on, he told them, the food they had paid for at Rotterdam would have to be paid for again. This time the price was much higher – he would only accept gold!

At the same time, he ordered the surviving crew members to search the baggage chests belonging to the passengers and stored out of their sight. From these, so it would appear, silver plate and other valuables were taken and shared out. Even if the Palatines on board reached America, they would be impoverished and quite unable to support themselves.

In mid-December the *Princess Augusta* finally came within sight of land. Brook, for his part, concluded that it was Maryland and dropping anchor he hoped soon to be rid of the passengers he was treating so badly. However, in reckoning the ship's position, he had failed to take into account the storms that had pushed him so far north. In fact, he was off Massachusetts. Before anyone could be disembarked Brook was forced towards midnight on December 19th, to weigh anchor again. Running before a northerly gale, he raced south, heading towards Long Island unable to find a safe haven. Then the wind backed to north-west and blew with an even greater viciousness, so that the mizzen mast snapped and some of the seams began to give, letting water leak into the hold.

Over Christmas the vessel remained marooned at sea. Distress signals were hoisted but these were unseen by those on shore. However, as she passed along the east side of Long Island, the wind finally died down.

Having now realised his earlier error, and aware that he was further north than he had first thought, an attempt was made to reach the safety of Narragansett Bay. Entering Block Island Sound from the south, the wind began to rise once again. This time it was accompanied by a blinding snow storm that cut visibility to only a few yards, so that they were unable to see how close they were to Block Island. The vessel finally struck at 2pm on December 26th 1738. Although she did work free some two hours later, it was only to result in her becoming more firmly entrenched in sands much closer to the island. On board the terrified passengers, desperate to get ashore, began to clamber along the bowsprit ready to drop down on the beach that lay immediately below. Brook, for his part, began to force them back.

News of the stranded ship soon circulated among the island community. A large number gathered on the beach and prepared to offer whatever comforts they could to those on board. However, they were more than a little concerned at the actions of Brook in not letting his passengers ashore. Eventually, Simon Ray, the chief government official on the island, was rowed over to the ship and took a note of the damage. Seeking out the former mate, he used the authority of his position, ordering that those passengers who wished to go ashore should be allowed to do so.

While those on board the *Princess Augusta* were making

their way ashore, Brook concerned himself with the cargo. Ensuring that none of the passengers took any of their own sea chests, he nevertheless hauled his own belongings on to the beach. It is now quite easy to discern his reasons for this strange move. His own chest contained many of the items previously looted, a fact of which the Palatine immigrants were blissfully unaware. If they had been allowed to take their own goods ashore many of them would have seen that they had been robbed. Clearly Brook was hoping that the vessel would soon break free, taking with her much of the evidence of his wrongdoing.

The islanders, for their part, had other ideas. Aware that the newly arrived immigrants had their life savings on board they were determined that as many chests as possible should be saved and returned to their rightful owners. For the purpose of securing the ship therefore, a cable was attached to the vessel. In addition, Simon Ray ordered the lowering of the heavy sheet anchor.

As the ill-treated passengers came ashore the placid islanders must have been truly shocked. Weak, emaciated and suffering a range of illnesses, some of them were so helpless that they simply lay on the sand, unable to move. At least two were to die within the next hour – cut down by the cruel north-west wind that continued to blow cold and damp from across the Atlantic.

Brook, still concerned with the necessity of hiding the evidence of his crimes, waited for high tide and cut the cable and anchor. Slowly, the vessel drifted away. On board, there remained one final passenger, a certain Mary Van der Line who had preferred not to be parted from her gold and silver. Nobody had realised that she failed to leave with the rest of the passengers.

With the onset of daylight, the Block Islanders were furious. How could Brook have acted in such a way? Deciding on one last bid to save some of the cargo, a number of them rowed after the drifting ship, boarded her, and took away twenty chests. Discovering the crazed Mary Van der Line, none of them were able to convince her that she ought to come ashore. As a result she was still on board the *Princess Augusta* when it crashed on to rocks at the south side of the island. Her body was never recovered.

While most of those rescued from the *Princess Augusta* eventually made the final stage of the journey to Philadelphia some chose to stay on Block Island. Perhaps, for the most part, these were the ones who could not afford to continue the journey having lost their life savings in the wreck. Entering into a completely different category however, was a tall handsome girl named Kattern, or Katherine. She appears to have fallen in love with New Port, a black slave named after the African town in which he had been born. It seems that New Port may have been responsible for rescuing Katherine from the stricken vessel, so helping their relationship to blossom.

Despite choosing to remain on Block Island, Katherine seems to have fallen out with most of the other islanders. As the result of some sort of grievance or misunderstanding, she started to accuse them of being responsible for wrecking the *Princess Augusta*. Over the following years, she frequently claimed that the residents of Block Island had deliberately lured the vessel on to Sandy Point before boarding the ship and stealing much of the cargo. Finally, so she might be heard to declare, they had set light to the ship, deliberately sending Mary Van der Line to her death.

Doubtless these stories would have been quickly forgotten had it not been for reports of a strange ghost ship that began to make a regular appearance off Block Island. According to a number of witnesses, the apparition took the form of a blazing ship that simply disappeared. The earliest witness to the sight was the captain of a trading vessel named *Somerset*. He reported the incident just one year after the loss of the *Princess Augusta*. According to his entry written into the ship's log: 'I was so distressed by the sight that we followed

the burning ship to her watery grave, but failed to find any
survivors or flotsam.'

More often however, the Block Island phantom seems to
have taken the form of a blazing light, with any ship that
might appear to be the cause remaining more or less invisible.
In 1811, an island resident wrote this account of the
phenomena:

> The light actually seen, sometimes one half mile
> from shore, where it lights up the walls of a gentle-
> man's rooms through the windows . . . The people
> here are so familiarised with the sight they never
> think of giving notice to those who do not happen
> to be present, or even mentioning it afterwards,
> unless they hear some particular enquiries have
> been made. It beams with various magnitudes.
> Sometimes it is small, resembling the light through
> a distant window, at others expanding to the light-
> ness of a ship with all her canvas spread. The blaze
> eventually emits luminous rays.

A number of published histories of Block Island also mention
the strange light, with numerous witnesses listed. Most
impressive is a late 19th century account that mentions
one islander having seen the phantom ship, or light, a total
of seven times. Numerous sightings have also been made
in more recent years. An article which appeared in a
1960 edition of *The Saturday Evening Post* quoted several
islanders who had seen the light. One of them explained
that it was normally associated with south-easterly winds.
In 1880, shortly after the light had been seen, a south
easterly storm ensued and claimed the lives of four yachts-
men.

The first reported appearance of the blazing ghost ship
having taken place so soon after the loss of the *Princess
Augusta* inevitably resulted in some people considering the
one to be the apparition of the other. In turn, this also gave

some credibilty to Katherine's version of events, for she was the one that claimed the *Princess Augusta* was burnt and not simply wrecked. As memories faded, and one generation followed another, the true story of events surrounding the loss of the *Princess Augusta* appears to have become totally forgotten. Instead, Katherine's fabricated story, supported as it was by many subsequent sightings of the strange light, became the accepted truth.

Something else also occurred with the passing of time. As the story of the wreck was handed down by word of mouth, many basic facts were also altered. By the mid-19th century, the vessel ceased being the *Princess Augusta* and had become the *Palatine*. Amongst those who gave it this particular name was Massachusetts born poet John Greenleaf Whittier. In 1867 he composed a ballad that clearly libelled the good people of Block Island, claiming their ancestors to have been wreckers who were in the habit of luring unsuspecting ships on to the island. In his poem, entitled *The Palatine*, Whittier seemed convinced that he was drawing upon historical fact rather than historical fiction:

> Into the teeth of death she sped
> (May God forgive the hands that fed
> The false lights over the rocky Head!
>
> O men and brothers! What sights were there!
> White upturned faces, hands stretched in prayers!
> Where waves had pity, could ye not spare?
>
> Down swooped the wreckers, like birds of prey.
> Tearing the heart of the ship away,
> And the dead had never a word to say.
>
> And then, with ghastly shimmer and shine
> Over the rocks and the seething brine,
> They burned the wreck of the Palatine.

In their cruel hearts, as they homeward sped,
'The sea and the rocks are dumb,' they said,
'They'll be no reckoning with the dead.'

But the year went round, and when once more
Along their foam-white curves of shore,
They heard the line-storm rave and roar,

Behold! Again, with a shimmer and a shine,
Over the rocks and the seething brine,
The flaming wreck of the Palatine!

A similar version of the story was given in a widely read and
seemingly well researched book, *The Phantom Ship*. Written
by R. L. Hadfield and published in 1937, it withholds few
punches when it comes to describing the unscrupulous nature
of the former residents of Block Island. Claiming the events
took place in 1752 (for by now the correct year had also been
forgotten), it is interesting to see how the story had been
further transformed since the writing of Whittier's poem. It
should, of course, also be noted that Hadfield also referred to
the *Princess Augusta* as the *Palatine*:

> There have been many wreckers in many lands,
> but those of Block Island were the most feared and
> detested of all.
>
> It was into the hands of these people that the
> *Palatine* and her passengers fell. The night grew
> dark, a stiff breeze sprang up, and the ship ap-
> proached nearer and nearer to the sinister island.
>
> According to some versions of this story the
> *Palatine* was accidentally cast ashore through the
> drunkeness of the seamen; others say that the cap-
> tain was in league with the wreckers of the island
> and purposely drove her ashore, knowing a point
> where she would ground in such a way that any
> who could handle the boats would be able to
> escape. With the knowledge that he would be shar-
> ing in the profits of the wreckers he had not con-

cerned himself with the robbing of the passengers, leaving that to his officers and men.

Whatever the cause, the *Palatine* drove ashore, and instantly there leapt upon her hundreds of wreckers, who, thrusting the passengers aside, flung themselves on the remnants of their baggage and the ship's stores, stripping her of all valuables, cutting down anyone who even accidentally got in their way, flinging the men into the sea, maltreating the women, behaving more like fiends than human beings.

The passengers were driven nearly mad with terror and despair. Was this the promised land? Was this the New England where fortune smiled and 'Liberty' was the watchword?

Many of them ran into the furtherest recesses of the ship, cowering there in their fear, whilst overhead they could hear the stamping of the wreckers' feet, their oaths and wild cries, and their shrieks of exultation as they dragged out the stores from the hold.

Later on, Hadfield goes on to refer to the fate of an unnamed passenger. She is, of course, the unfortunate Mary Van der Line who now appears to have acquired a babe in arms:

> ... In the indescribable confusion and uproar she had lost the babe she had brought with her from Europe, and now, overcome with sorrow and terror, she crouched in a dark corner below decks.
>
> Suddenly, to her ears came a strange sound, a crisp, crackling sound which slowly developed into a roar. She raised her head and listened, wondering what new terror this sound might portend. Then there came a burst of light from above her head, and she knew at last what was happening. The ship was on fire. Stripped in an hour or two, she was now a useless hulk and evidence of the perpetration of a great crime. The wreckers of

Block Island wished to see her no more, and, fired fore and aft, she was beginning to blaze to the heavens.

The unhappy woman saw her danger as the flames began to burst through the bulkheads. She roused herself, and by the light of the fire found her way on deck. Not far off was the shore, covered with the twinkling lights of the wreckers lanterns and firebrands, but between her and them raged the flames that were gutting the Palatine. Screaming she ran to the poop, cordage all afire falling round her as she ran. But there was no escape there. Mad with terror, driven out of her mind by her sufferings, the woman leapt on to the bulwarks and stood there screaming to those on shore to give her back her baby, her figure silhouetted against the fiery background.

But she was past help. None, even if he wished, could have reached her and snatch her from the furnace, and as the wreckers watched, they suddenly saw the victim of their avarice fall from the bulwark and disappear into the flaming cauldron of fire in the heart of the ship.

The frequent reiteration of such accusations against those from whom they were descended eventually led a few Block Islanders to attempt to find out just how much of all this was true. Were their ancestors 'the most feared and detested of all' wreckers? Was it not possible to say a single good word about the earliest settlers on Block Island?

The first person to carry out any form of historical investigation was the Rev. Samuel T. Livermore, island pastor towards the end of the 19th century. During his period of service on the island he had given some attention to the story, interviewing a number of his older parishioners. Although none of them, of course, remembered the original incident, they did indicate that stories had long been current of a ship having been wrecked on the island and how their parents had told them of attempts to help those on board. Further progress was not made until 1925 when Elizabeth Dickens, a direct descendant of one of the original families to settle on the island, began a search of the Rhode Island state archives. It was her efforts that resulted in the correct date and name of the ship being unearthed.

Perhaps the most important breakthrough in setting the record straight was the discovery of various contemporary documents that referred to the *Princess Augusta* running aground. In the Rhode Island archives sworn statements, made by those on board the *Princess Augusta* were discovered. In addition, a number of contemporary newspaper reports were also unearthed. These, between them, not only proved the Block Islanders to be innocent of the many crimes they were accused, but they also told of the treatment that Andrew Brook had meted out to his passengers.

The earliest report of the *Princess Augusta* appeared in *The Boston Weekly Newsletter* issued for the period January 11th to 18th, 1739:

> We are informed by Letter from Block-Island, dated the first Instant, to the Hon. John Wanton, Esq; our Governour, That a large ship of about 300 Tons: was cast away on said Island the 26th of December last; she was very Rich, reckon'd to be worth Twenty Thousand Pounds Sterling; she came from Rotterdam last August, but last from Cowes in England, having on board 340 Palatine Passengers and Servants bound to Philadelphia; but having a long Passage, near 200 died while on it; the Remainder came on Shore, and 20 of them are dead since they came on the island.
>
> Their captain, whose name was Long, died in the Passage, and his Mate took the Charge of the Ship as Captain and Commander, after the said Long's death; and he being often desired by some of the Gentlemen of the Island, to suffer the Pas-

sengers to take their Goods out of the Ship, he
absolutely refused it; tho' many of them saved
their Silver and Gold. Tho' all possible means were
used to prevent clandestine Actions, many have
lost by Extortion and other ways, a great Part of
the little which they saved.

A more detailed account of the events occurring on Block
Island appeared in *The Boston Gazette* edition for mid-
March. The report began with references to those on the
island begging Andrew Brook to allow the chests and other
items to be brought off the ship:

> ... which he would not comply with, tho' at the
> same Time he told he had fifteen thousand weight
> of Bread on board, but could not answer breaking
> of bulk; and he had got all the Goods belonging to
> himself and Sailors on shore. But the greatest diffi-
> culty was in transporting those objects of Pity,
> carrying some in Blankets, some on Mens backs,
> others on Horses (the Snow being deep) to two
> Cottages, a Mile from the Ship, the most of those
> People being sick, froze and starved, and two of
> the Women were froze to Death on the Beach
> before our People came to their Assistance; the
> next Day many of our People went to said Ship,
> and was told the Ship floated in the Night, and
> waited the Captain's coming ashore, whom the
> Officer here as well as many of the Inhabitants,
> again importuned with him, to have compassion
> on those distressed Objects, in giving them Bread
> &c. having eat nothing in two Days, and also to
> suffer their Goods to be brought on shore, which
> Request he did not absolutely deny, but said he
> could not spare his Boat, nor any of his Men, he
> having occasion for them in saving the Tackling of
> said Ship; he was answered by the Officers &c. if
> he would give leave they would get on shore their
> Goods &c. he said he had more regard to the

saving said Tackling &c. than in saving the Palatines Goods, and little or nothing was done; in the
meantime, the Distressed greatly suffered, being
obliged to go 4, 5, 6 Miles, to get them Provisions,
no Inhabitants being nearer. The Captain did
order to unbend the Cable from the aforesaid Anchor (as his Men and others whom he employed
testify) and the next Day the Ship was a-drift with
all the Palatines Goods and Money &c. and by
several we are informed with two living Souls.
Some of the Neighbours went in a small Vessel on
board said Ship, and took out 20 Chests with a
considerable quantity of their Goods, which were
brought on shore and housed; and the next day the
said Ship came on shore on the west side of the
Island, where she stove to pieces.

As for the sworn deposition, these entirely support the published newspaper accounts. As well as this, they also provide
evidence of Andrew Brook's nefarious activities, including
strong hints of his having rifled property belonging to the
Palatine immigrants. More important, from the point of view
of those living on Block Island, was that one of these documents prove, without a shadow of a doubt, that the *Princess
Augustus* was not lured to the island by wreckers. According
to two crew members, in a statement sworn before Simon Ray
on January 11th 1739:

> Then we stear'd away W. S. W. & S. W. by Wt to
> go between Block Island and Long Island and it
> was so exceeding thick of Snow the wind about N.
> N. Et. We could not see much above three times
> the length of the said Ship and about two of the
> Clock the said Captain Andrew Brook saw
> Something loom as a cloud and instantly ordered
> the Helme hard a Port But before it could be done
> the Ship struck the Shore & struck fast And in
> about two Hours after justl'd off But had not got

above three times her Length before she struck
again and struck very hard and beat a piece
of Plank off the Bottom Eight or nine feet
long . . .

Informative as the various newspaper reports and re-dis-
covered documents might be, none of them get anywhere
near to suggesting a likely explanation of that essential aspect
of the *Princess Augusta* wreck – that of her suggested spectre.
Given that the vessel did not end her days in a fiery blaze, then
it seems unreasonable to connect her with that particular
phenomenon. Instead, we must look elsewhere for a likely
cause.

Over the years, several possible explanations have been
put forward. Most have tended to ignore the possibility
of it being anything to do with a burning ship and have
concentrated on various types of natural phenomena. One
frequent suggestion is that the blazing light is a form of St
Elmo's fire. This is an electrical manifestation that only
occurs during certain atmospheric conditions, such as when
a storm is in the offing. St Elmo's fire would certainly explain why the light tends to be associated with rising winds.
Flashing across the yardarms and masthead of a ship, this
brush-like electrical discharge has a brightness much akin
to the light which has made a not infrequent appearance off
Block Island. In olden times sailors used to think that this
natural phenomenon was a manifestation of the supernatural.

A second suggestion put forward is that the light results
from gases rising to the surface. Again, if a storm is within the
area, then these gases may be ignited by lightning. Such a
manifestation would happen fairly infrequently, but when it
did occur the resulting flame would certainly be bright enough
to illuminate a book or newspaper.

As for the Block Islanders, they are quite happy to foster a
continued belief in the light and its supernatural connections.

After all, with the supposed sin of an earlier generation now disproved, it does provide an additional arm to a fairly profitable tourist trade.

New-Port, Rhode Island January 1, 1738 9.

We are informed by a Letter from Block-Island, dated the first Instant, to the Hon. John Wanton, Esq; our Governour, That a large Ship of about 300 Tuns was cast away on said Island the 16th December last; she was very Rich, reckon'd to be worth Twenty Thousand Pounds Sterling; she came from Rotterdam last August, but last from Cowes in England, having on board 340 Palatine Passengers and Servants bound to Philadelphia; but having a long Passage near 200 of them died while on it; the Remainder came on Shore, and 20 of them are dead since they came on the Island

Their Captain, whose Name was Long, died in the Passage, and his Mate took the Charge of the Ship as Captain and Commander, after the said Long's Death; and he being often desired by some of the Gentlemen of the Island, to suffer the Passengers to take their Goods out of the Ship, He absolutely refused it; tho' many of them saved their Silver and Gold: Tho' all possible Means were used to prevent clandestine Actions, many have lost by Extortion and other ways, a great Part of the little which they saved.

After the Ship broke to pieces there were abundance of Goods came ashore, but theOwners cannot have any of them, without paying a third Salvage, besides which a great Part of them are confiscated, together with greatQuantities of Silver and Gold: In short, Tongue and Pen cannot relate the present Circumstances of the poor Palatines, whose Number is said to be but only 85 Persons.

Upon this melancholy News our Governour sent a Magistrate and other proper Officers to Block-Island, to see how Matters are, that those poor People may have Justice done them.

A report from the front page of *The Boston Weekly News-Letter* for the first half of January 1739. Describing the *Princess Augusta* running aground on Block Island. It is this vessel that gave rise to a number of enduring legends.

Chatham during the mid-nineteenth century. Could this be the world's most haunted dockyard? Among the buildings at Chatham said to be haunted is its unique 18th century rope-house, pictured below. Here, during the age of fighting sail, rigging was manufactured for the Royal Navy's warships.

14

The haunted dockyard and other naval ghost stories

The Royal Navy has been in continual existence for approximately 500 years. During this time, its ships have been involved in every imaginable enterprise. It has fought battles in all the oceans of the globe, safeguarded the far-flung British Empire, helped rid the world of both pirates and slavers or given aid and succour to the survivors of shipwreck, earthquake and other natural disasters.

With such a long and proud history it can be of no surprise to learn that this mighty force has often seen its ranks enlarged by the recruitment of ghosts and others from the supernatural world. For the most part, they do not choose to join their old ships, but prefer to take up residence in the ports from which they sailed or were once closely connected.

Proving a particular attraction for the maritime ghost is the former naval town of Chatham, England. It was here, from the 16th century onwards, that a large number of the nation's warships were built and repaired. Here vessels with such illustrious names as *Victory*, *Renown* and *Temeraire*, were launched into the River Medway. Because of these activities, and the existence of a nearby naval barracks, thousands of officers and ratings, including many famous admirals, passed through the dockyard gates.

The yard, itself has in recent years met its own peculiar fate. Abandoned by the Royal Navy in 1984, it has subsequently been thrown into the tourist market, attracting more than 100,000 people each year. Visitors are given free range over a multi-acre site once dedicated to Britain's 'wooden walls'. In fact, the yard is now a living museum, with craftsmen employed to demonstrate their ancient skills, a working rope walk, sail loft and other workshops.

These various attractions are, of course, relatively well advertised. Less well known are the frequent, if somewhat unpredictable activities, of the supernatural residents of the yard. In February 1990, it was reported in the local papers that staff employed in the Visitors' Centre were shocked by the antics of a heavy glass jar. For no apparent reason it suddenly flew across the room, scattering its content of badges when it smashed ten feet away on the floor.

This bizarre incident happened under bright lights and in front of four witnesses. Although nobody has come up with a definitive explanation, the episode was commonly believed to have had something to do with poltergeists. A poltergeist is defined by the Oxford English Dictionary as a 'noisy and mischievous spirit', and such a one might have been connected with the building's earlier use as galvanising shop. Here, from the late-1890s onwards, workers were employed in preparing the zinc used to protect warships against rust and it is not inconceivable that the spirit of one former employee has gained some strange attachment to the building.

Yet this is only one of many ghosts that are to be found within the dockyard's perimeter. At the end of the day, with the building otherwise empty, footsteps have been heard coming from the deserted first floor of the yard's 18th century ropehouse. Those responsible for locking the building have usually found nothing out of the ordinary, although on one occasion an actual ghost seems to have been witnessed. This took the form of a young boy who appeared to be dressed in the clothes of an earlier age. On being approached, this spirit, or whatever it might have been, reportedly disappeared.

Again, such a presence may not be unconnected with the use of this building in earlier times. Erected during the 1780s, and used for the spinning and laying of rope used in the rigging of warships, those employed on these tasks included a small number of youngsters. According to a report dated 1810, and which examined work methods used in the rope-walk, some of these children were only eight years of age.

Towards the centre of the historic dockyard stands an interesting three storey building that also dates back to the 18th century. Known as the Clock Tower building, for it has a simple bell tower and clock projecting from the centre of its roof, this also has a strange reputation. It appears that the clock tower itself may well be haunted. People entering into this more confined area have been subjected to sudden and unexpected noises and the movement of objects close at hand.

The yard's most famous ghost however, is that of Admiral Horatio Nelson. Although not normally associated with the dockyard at Chatham, Nelson does have some important connections with the area. Not least of these is the fact that HMS *Victory*, his famous flagship, was actually built at the yard, being laid down on the orders of Prime Minister Pitt in 1759 and so named because that was 'the year of victories' for British armed forces.

However if Nelson, as has been claimed, does walk the ancient stone pathways of Chatham's royal dockyard, it is most likely a result of his having initially come to this port as a young lad when about to join his first ship. This was during the year 1770 when *Raisonnable*, then under the command of Maurice Suckling, Nelson's uncle, was preparing for sea. Nelson, having shown an interest in joining the Navy, had been invited to join his uncle's ship as a midshipman. If, therefore, Nelson can be said to have had a spiritual home, then Chatham must surely be one of the obvious choices, for it was from this port that the world's most famous admiral first sailed.

It might be noted that the vision of Admiral Nelson witnessed in the dockyard was not of the visually handicapped and one armed personage with which most people are familiar. Instead, it is of the younger man prior to the siege of

Calvi (where he was blinded in the right eye) and the attempted seizure of a Spanish treasure ship at Santa Cruz (when he lost his right arm). Perhaps, indeed, the figure is so unlike Nelson, that certain over-enthusiastic assumptions have been made by past witnesses. Naval officer this presence may be, but the most esteemed of all naval heroes . . .

Most of the Chatham sightings so far described have all taken place in more recent years. However, there is evidence that the dockyard has been a haven for ghosts for over 300 years. On April 8th 1661 the famous diarist Samuel Pepys, made an inspection of the dockyard. At the time he was Secretary to the Navy Board and it was his task to report on the efficiency of the various officers employed at Chatham. During such visits it was the practice for Navy Board officers to be accommodated in Hill House, the yard's official residence. According to Pepys's diary the evening proved fairly eventful:

> 'Then to the Hill House at Chatham, where I never was before, and I found a pretty pleasant house, and am pleased with the armes that hang up there. Here we supped very merry, and late to bed; Sir William telling me that old Edgebarrow, his predecessor, did die and walk in my chamber, did make me somewhat afraid, but not so much as for merth's sake I did seem. So to bed in the Treasurer's chamber. Lay and slept till three in the morning, and then waking and by the light of the moon I saw my pillow (which overnight I flung from me) stand upright, but not bethinking myself what it might be I was a little afraid, but sleep overcame all, and so lay till nigh morning, at which time I had a candle brought me, and a good fire made, and in general it was great pleasure all the time I stayed here . . .'

Another of the ghosts from Chatham dockyard seems to have caused something of a commotion during World War Two.

At that time the dockyard was busily engaged in the vital role of refitting numerous warships. As both the yard and the adjoining naval barracks were both potential targets for German bombers, it was decided that one of the terraced houses, normally reserved for yard officers and their families, should be turned into a mess for medical staff. It so happens that the particular house chosen, No.9, was also the one reckoned by many to be haunted by a friendly ghost. Although little is remembered about the pre-war activities of this particular ghost, it would seem that the newly installed naval doctors found it to be a spirit with an unusual sense of humour.

Once the new medical mess had been fitted out it became customary for a duty doctor to sleep there overnight, available to treat any injuries sustained by those working on the nightshift. If such an accident occurred, then one of the sick bay attendants would go over to the terrace and knock on the duty doctor's door. It appears that several of the doctors spoke of being 'knocked up' only to find that when they reached the surgery, they were not needed and that nobody had been sent to summon them.

On one occasion a relief mess commander was given accommodation in the sick bay. Offered the choice of two rooms, he was told that the first room was best avoided as it was the one most frequented by the ghost. Refusing to countenance the idea of the house being haunted, he resolutely chose the room about which he had been warned. This proved to be a mistake!

As he attempted to settle down for a good night's rest, he found his thoughts disturbed by the sound of footsteps coming from the room above. Upon inspecting the room however, he found it to be completely empty. Returning to his own room, the footsteps were once again clearly audible. The disturbances continued into the small hours of the morning, so it can hardly come as a surprise to learn that the relief commander chose the second of the two proffered rooms for

In Devonport's Fore Street can be found Aggie Weston's, a haunted sailor's rest.

In the dockyard at Chatham it seems likely that the clocktower, standing over a former store-house, is also haunted. Within sight of this building, Nelson's *Victory* was constructed.

Pembroke dockyard at the turn of the century. On either side of the main entrance are to be seen a set of officers' houses. As with the dockyard at Chatham, one of them appears to be haunted. (Photo Phil Carradice)

A particularly well documented ghost appears to have haunted a former officer's house within Chatham dockyard. The house concerned, No 9, is the one fronted by the second porch from the right.

the remainder of his period of duty in the Chatham dockyard medical mess.

Chatham is not the only dockyard town or port that can lay claim to a series of ghosts with naval connections. At Portsmouth, a town virtually synonymous with the British navy, assurances are given that another batch of ghosts, all connected in some way with the high seas, either once existed or still continue to exist.

It is, of course, highly likely that HMS *Victory*, both the Royal Navy's and Portsmouth's greatest monument (not withstanding that the vessel was built at Chatham) may itself be haunted. After all, thousands of seamen have passed through her decks, 57 of whom were killed during the Battle of Trafalgar. How likely is it, therefore, that this famous ship should house a discontented spirit?

However, it is Portsmouth Point, the area of land outside Portsmouth dockyard's main gate that is particularly worthy of consideration. Here, there once stood an impressive inn whose name was indelibly emblazoned upon the hearts of many an officer of the sailing navy whose younger years were spent in this port. The hostelry concerned was *The Blue Posts* in Broad Street, an institution in its own right and particularly a favourite haunt of midshipmen.

Memories of this former coaching inn, for it was from here that the London coach made its daily departure, are recalled by M. H. Barker, a midshipman during the Napoleonic Wars. In later years he used some of his memories in the writing of *Jem But: A Tale of the Land and the Ocean*. Of the 'dear delightful Blue Posts', he once wrote 'how well do I remember your characteristic columns at the entrance, and the snug coffee-room on the right-hand side of the passage; happy and joyous have been the hours I have passed within those walls – many a bleak winter morning have I had charge of the large cutter, and pulled or sailed in from Spithead, shivering with cold – wet, hungry and fretful.'

Another who formed a strong attachment with *The Blue*

Posts was Captain Marryat, a famous author of books of naval fiction. In one of these his hero, Peter Simple, is told by the coachman that it was at this inn that midshipmen 'left their chestesses, called for tea and toastesses, and sometimes forgot to pay for their breakfastesses'. It is however, to another writer, the Rev. Richard Harris Barham, that we need to turn for evidence of *The Blue Posts* being haunted. Barham, whom we have already met under his nom-de-plume Thomas Ingoldsby, the author of *The Ingoldsby Legends*, outlines a peculiarly fascinating story in his diary, claiming it to be 'one of the best authenticated ghost stories in existence'.

Sometime towards the end of the 18th century a certain Mr Hamilton was brought to the crowded town of Portsmouth. Several naval ships had recently arrived and many of their discharged crews were wandering the streets in a state of intoxication. Hamilton, not wishing to be part of this, took a room for the night at 'The Blue Posts', insisting that he did not wish to be disturbed. To this end, indeed, he secured the door from the inside, satisfying himself that nobody could possibly enter.

Sometime during the night he was awoken by the sounds of a general commotion coming from the lane that ran immediately under his window. This caused him to turn over and at this point he noticed that a previously unoccupied second bed in the room was now very definitely occupied. Somewhat surprised, and annoyed that the landlady had broken an agreement that allowed him sole use of the room, he decided it would be best to leave the matter until later.

In the morning, when Hamilton eventually awoke he was in a position to observe his still slumbering companion. As the Rev. Mr Barham was later informed, the man appeared to be a sailor. Leastways he was wearing clothes typical of those following this profession, while his most distinctive feature was a bushy black beard covering much of his face. More disturbing, from Hamilton's point of view, was that the man also wore a white headscarf partly saturated in blood. Clearly, the man had been involved in a fight!

Obviously, Hamilton was a little concerned as to how the man had gained entry. He had certainly locked the door the previous night and the key, which he had left on the inside of the lock, was still in place. For this reason he decided he ought to quiz the man, but turning, once again, to face the bed, he discovered to his utter amazement that the occupant of the bed had disappeared.

Turning the entire matter over in his mind, he decided he would confront the landlady. At the very least she owed him some money, for he had paid the sum she had requested for exclusive use of the room and it was most unfair on her part, to let it to a second guest. Well, to cut a long story short, the landlady firmly denied that she had let anyone else in. As evidence, she reminded Hamilton that, by his own admission, he had securely locked the room. Moreover, there was not, as Hamilton had thought likely, some hidden second entrance.

Before letting the matter drop Hamilton threw in his final card. He chose to describe the man, emphasising those thick black whiskers. At this point, so the story goes, the landlady paled. 'Lord have mercy upon me!' she cried out. Finally, she offered the only possible explanation. The man, so she claimed, must have been one of a party of sailors who had spent sometime drinking at the inn a few nights earlier. All had been recently discharged from returning warships and were celebrating the end of a long period at sea. As often happens in such situations, one group got into an argument with another. Despite her attempted intervention, drinking pots, chairs and tables were all upturned and thrown.

Involved in the fight were a party of marines. They seemed viciously intent upon wounding a particular party of sailors who had just completed service on board a rival ship. Treating their opponents as if they were engaged in a battle at sea with a foreign foe, the marines eventually felled a young bewhiskered matelot who had been fairly active in the fighting. It was clear that the man was badly injured. Blood was pouring from a head wound and attempts to staunch the flow with a white handkerchief proved little more than useless. The landlady, offering what help she could, allowed him to be carried to the same upstairs room as that later to be occupied by Hamilton. Lying on the second bed in the room, the man lasted but a few hours and died that same night.

In an attempt to keep the matter secret, so that nobody would get into trouble, it was decided that the body should be buried in the garden. As the landlady now realised, raising her eyes to the heavens above, all had been in vain. The restless spirit of the murdered man had returned to take his revenge.

A far more recent ghost story is attached to HMS *Mercury*, a naval training establishment that lies just 16 miles north of Portsmouth. At any one time there are 60 officers and 500 naval ratings based there, most of the latter preparing for a career in the communications branch of the Silent Service. Although part of *Mercury* is centred around an older building, a new section to the establishment was added during the 1960s. This was Eagle Block, a group of rather functional matchbox shaped buildings, that have about as much character as a cement barge on the River Thames. However, Eagle Block, appears to have something which many older and more characterful buildings lack, it has a ghost.

Apparently, it is the spirit of a young WRNS rating who died while the building was under construction. In February 1961, while going about her normal duties, she was struck by falling masonry. Seriously injured, she was rushed to hospital but died shortly afterwards.

Ever since that unfortunate incident, Eagle Block has been associated with numerous inexplicable happenings. For a start, it is not uncommon for reports to be made of a young woman apparently trapped in one of the rooms, her face sometimes being seen at the window. Upon investigation, the particular room is unlocked and always found to be empty. Something else that can not be explained is why Eagle Block is always considerably colder than any of the other buildings fed by the same heating system.

As evidence of something being not quite right with this building, take this report which appeared in the Royal Navy's *Communicator* magazine and which refers to an incident that occurred on Saturday July 10th 1976:

> On that night, at 2150, the foot patrol reported a light on in Eagle block – 26 classroom – despite the fact that rounds had been going on all day and nobody had seen it previously. At 2152 the patrol entered the block and reported hearing noises upstairs. At 2200 the leading hand of the Emergency Party went to assist and at 2205 the Firefly was called out to illuminate the roof. The Petty Officer of the Guard found the roof door open and it was assumed that an intruder had broken into the block. At 2207 a light came on in the Wrens Heads, and the Firefly driver reported possible movements upstairs in the block. At 2228, after a complete search of the block had drawn a blank, the block was secured. The light in Classroom 26 was left in the on position as the 'pull cord' had broken off when the patrol had tried to switch it off. At 2333 the patrol reported the light had mysteriously switched itself off.

It would seem that all of Britain's naval towns have a haunting of one type or another. In Plymouth, in earlier years, the famous 'Aggie Weston's' had a ghost that would occasionally make its presence felt to those who stayed overnight. For those unfamiliar with Miss Agatha Weston and her rest homes, it should be mentioned that these were temperance centres designed to act as a counter-attraction to the many pubs and brothels that were always to be found in the Victorian naval towns. These homes which provided reading rooms, games facilities and cheap food were very popular with naval ratings, as they gave them the opportunity of a change from life aboard or in the local barracks with its frequently harsh and uncompromising rules. It was the earliest of these 'Aggie Weston's', established in Devonport's Fore Street, to which this particular ghost appears to have become attached.

A further town with naval and dockyard connections is Pembroke. Elsewhere, in this book, reference has been made to *Asp*, a Royal Navy survey vessel that, upon entering the dockyard at Pembroke, was able to rid herself of a rather unwelcome female apparition. However, this is not the only ghost that has found its way into the Pembroke dockyard area. It appears that one of the dockyard buildings acquired its own supernatural presence.

The particular building, once an officer's residence but now become a hotel, since Pembroke dockyard was closed in 1947, was originally built for use by those in command of the dockyard. As those who now operate the hotel will confirm, some rooms have pronounced cold spots. But this is far from being the only proof of it being haunted. On other occasions guests have commented on seeing a serving girl, always accompanied by the smell of lavender, who simply glides through a set of French windows located in what is now the TV room. Upon asking members of the staff who she may be they are informed that there is no member of staff fitting that particular description.

Indeed there is no obvious clue to her identity. The dockyard officers, who once occupied this building, would certainly have had their own servants. It is not improbable, therefore, that this particular apparition dates back to the days when Pembroke yard was employed in the building of ocean going warships and the serving girl an indispensable member of the household team.

Further evidence of the supernatural at work within the confines of Pembroke dockyard comes from Arthur Samuel, a former sailor whose normal duties took him to this port. On one occasion, during the 1970s, with his own vessel tied to a trot mooring close to the floating jetty known as *C.77* (in reality the former ironclad HMS *Warrior*, since restored and transferred to Portsmouth), he found himself observing an unmanned and darkened boat. Moving at a steady speed, but completely unaided by either engine or sail, the observed vessel's progress was, nevertheless, somehow controlled. Even more frightening, from Samuel's point of view, was that not a sound emanated from the craft. It was as if the vessel was not really there!

Although it was night time, Arthur Samuel appears to have got a good view of this strange sight, it having been drawn into a pool of light shed by the moored vessel. At the time, he reckoned the craft to have been about 15ft to 20ft in length. Its progression not even marked by a bow wave.

Arthur Samuel also recalls a further unusual incident which took place in Pembroke Dock. This time it was during the afternoon when the crew were off duty and Samuel had retired to his bunk. More or less as soon as he had pulled the curtain across, a photograph of a man dramatically appeared! As Samuel later explained, the picture was still in a wooden frame and showed the head and shoulders of a man in military uniform. Although he was unable to put a name to the face, it was clear that it showed someone from the 19th century. The man had a high stiff-necked collar and a great deal of braid. Samuel also described him as handsome with stern features. As the surprised seaman lay there, the photograph moved backwards and forwards about six times before finally disappearing.

Moving away from the dockyard towns, it seems that the Royal Naval College at Greenwich possibly boasts a former admiral as a resident ghost. Apparently a frock coated figure has been seen in various corridors of the building, while others have heard footsteps coming from rooms that, upon investigation, are found to be empty. It is also a fact that some of the female cleaners refuse to enter a number of rooms in the building, declaring that there is something strange and unusual about them.

Although definite evidence is lacking, it has been suggested that the building might be haunted by Admiral John Byng who was sentenced by a court martial to be shot by a firing squad on the quarterdeck of HMS *Monarch* on March 14th 1747. His crime was that of failing to press home attacks on a French fleet lying off Minorca?

Modern naval historians tend to the view that his death was really a political expedient. Other, earlier admirals, could certainly be accused of similar failings, but their actions had not coincided with administrative inefficiencies that, in themselves had already allowed French forces to gain a foothold on the previously British held island of Minorca.

The connection between Byng and the college buildings is fairly tenuous. Prior to his execution, when these same buildings were part of a naval hospital, the admiral was imprisoned in one of the more isolated rooms. If the apparition, as described, is that of the admiral, then it can only be assumed that he is desperately trying to free himself from both imprisonment and the ignominy of the court martial and its unjust verdict.

A far more likely possibility, given that the building once served as a naval hospital, is that the ghostly sounds and occasionally glimpsed frock coated figure, is that of a former inmate. Over the years hundreds of seamen, injured in battle or in some peace time accident, were brought to the hospital, where they served out their final moments. Is it not more likely, given Byng's rather limited connection with Greenwich, that the figure seen is one of these lesser known individuals, rather than that of the ill-famed loser in the battle for Minorca?

Another naval ghost is that of Admiral Sir George Tryon. This is a particularly interesting story as it tells of a spectre that never existed. Nobody has ever seen the ghost of Admiral Tryon nor has its presence been detected through a sudden fall in room temperature, the sound of his voice or the steady pitter-patter of his footsteps. Quite simply, despite the claims of more than a dozen writers of ghost books, this one phantom has never appeared. In fact, the ghost of Admiral Sir George Tryon is a complete fabrication.

Admiral Sir George Tryon died on the bridge of his flagship HMS *Victoria* in very mysterious circumstances. While in command of the Mediterranean Fleet he ordered his own ship, and the flagship of Admiral Markham, who was his second-in-command, to turn inwards upon one another, for the purpose of reversing direction. As both vessels were on a parallel course, and separated by a mere 1,200 yds, they had less than the required distance for the proper performance of such a manoeuvre. Despite being reminded by subordinates of this fact Admiral Tryon failed to rescind the order until it was too late. As a result, there was a quite horrendous collision in which *Victoria* was struck on the starboard bow. Damage inflicted on the flagship was made considerably worse by virtue of the second ship, HMS *Camperdown*, having a lethal underwater ram, designed for the purpose of disabling enemy warships through means of deliberate collision. The ram penetrated nine feet into *Victoria*'s hull. A resulting flood of water soon ensured the loss of Tryon's flagship which went down with the admiral refusing to leave the bridge. A total of 385 lives were lost.

The reason for Admiral Tryon giving such an inexplicable instruction has never been satisfactorily answered. Various suggestions have been put forward, ranging from the onset of mental illness through to a misguided attempt at testing his second-in-command's ability to take independent action when obedience to a given order would endanger the fleet. I have examined this mysterious collision between *Victoria* and *Camperdown* in more detail in my earlier book *Mysteries on the High Seas*.

It was at the very moment of Admiral Tryon's death that his

Chatham dockyard's most famous ghost is that of Admiral Horatio Nelson.

Admiral Tryon. His ghost is widely believed to have appeared in London at a time coinciding with his death in the Mediterranean.

The final moments of the battleship HMS *Victoria*.

ghost is said to have made its appearance in the family home which was then situated in London's Eaton Square. A number of slightly differing versions of this event are to be found, but virtually all of them agree that Lady Tryon was entertaining a number of guests who had been invited to a party. Although she herself is not reported to have seen the ghost, the presence of Admiral Tryon within the house was quickly reported to her. In recognising the admiral, who was in full dress uniform, those who saw him were somewhat puzzled, all of them realizing that he was then in the Mediterranean. Indeed, none, at this stage, believed they were witnessing a ghost.

As with so many books on ghost stories, few of the writers choose to give a source. In most cases, an earlier written account is simply regurgitated with no attempt seemingly made to check its veracity. Sometimes, as with the *Ellen Austin* affair, the original account is even 'improved' with a certain amount of embroidering. This certainly appears to have been the case with regard to the much repeated claim of Admiral Sir George Tryon appearing at his Eaton Square home at roughly the moment of his death.

Of the numerous accounts given, only one of them offers any possible source. This is Will Eisner's *Spirit Casebook of True Haunted Houses and Ghosts*. Claiming that the story first appeared in the August 1893 edition of *Review of Reviews*, Eisner informs his readers that after Tryon had been seen by a number of guests at the party, they duly informed Lady Tryon. Running towards the library, the room in which he supposedly appeared, she found it to be empty. However, on the globe that stood to one side of the room, a moist fingerprint was visible. Amazingly, it marked a point in the Mediterranean – the exact point where the two ships had collided. Of even greater significance was a wet footprint behind the admiral's desk and the fact that the clock in this room had stopped at 3.44, the time when the collision occurred.

Melvin Harris, an investigator of ghost stories, chose to test out Eisner's claims, turning to the August 1893 edition of *Review of Reviews*. Harris found that there was, very definitely, a reference to that strange incident in the Mediterranean, but not one single word devoted to Tryon's apparition having appeared in London. If such a story was current, then *Review of Reviews* would certainly have carried it because, as mentioned in the chapter detailing the various forewarnings that affected many of those travelling on board the *Titanic*, the periodical was edited by W. T. Stead, a man with a particular interest in the supernatural.

It is, of course, always possible that Eisner made a mistake when listing the particular edition of *Review of Reviews*. As a result, Harris took his investigation a little further, checking several further editions. Although no further references were found to Admiral Tryon, Harris did come upon an interesting story that appeared in the Christmas 1892 issue. Written for the purpose of pure entertainment, and claimed to be nothing more than fiction, the story, entitled *A Ghost in a Ballroom*, told of a man who made an appearance at a party but failed to talk to anyone. Only later was it realised that, at the moment of the appearance, the man had been many miles away, having just drowned himself. The story also includes a reference to a watch stopping at the time of death.

The conclusions, according to Harris, are inescapable. Eisner was the originator of the Tryon ghost story. Admiral Sir George Tryon did not miraculously make an appearance in his Eaton Square house. Instead, the reference made to *Review of Reviews* was simply a ruse to give credibility to an interesting story. It would seem that Eisner was a keen reader of this particular periodical and somehow confused, or chose to confuse, two completely different stories. As for the later writers who referred to this 'famed' ghost, they are guilty of nothing more than failing to check their facts.

Bibliography

Archibald, Grace, *The Truth About the Titanic* (Conn., USA 1980)

Armstrong, Warren, *Sea Phantoms* (London, 1964)

Barnaby, K. C., *Some Ship Disasters and their Causes* (London, 1968)

Beesley, Lawrence, *The Loss of the SS Titanic* (Boston, 1912)

Beke, G., *Titanic, Psychic Forewarnings of a Tragedy* (USA, 1986).

Beresford, C., *The Memoirs of Admiral Lord Charles Beresford* (London, 1914)

Berlitz, Charles, *The Bermuda Triangle Mystery* (New York, 1974)

Brown, Rustie, *The Titanic, the Psychic and the Sea* (Lomita, California, 1981)

Burdett, *The Odyssey of an Orchid Hunter* (London 1930)

Canning, John (ed), *50 Strange Mysteries of the Sea* (London, 1979)

Cohen, Daniel, *Encyclopedia of Ghosts* (London, 1984)

de la Croix, Robert, *Mysteries of the Pacific* (London, 1957)

Dugan, James, *The Great Iron Ship* (New York, 1953)

Dumpleton, B., and Miller, M., *Brunel's Three Ships* (1982)

Edwards, Frank *Strangest of All* (New York, 1956)

Ellison, N., *Wirral Peninsula* (1955)

Emmerson, G. S., *SS Great Eastern* (Newton Abbot, 1980)

Eunson, Keith, *The Wreck of the General Grant* (Wellington, NZ, 1974)

Gaddis, Vincent, *Invisible Horizons* (Radnor, Pa, USA, 1965)

Garrett, Richard, *Voyage into Mystery* (London, 1987)

Gould, R. L., *The Stargazer Talks* (London, 1944)

Greenhouse, Herbert B., *Premonitions: A Leap into the Future* (London, 1971)

Hadfield, R. L., *The Phantom Ship* (London, 1937)

Hallam, Jack, *The Ghosts Whose Who* (Newton Abbot, 1977)

Harris, Melvin, *Investigating the Unexplained* (New York, 1986)

Hines, Terence, *Pseudoscience and the Paranormal* (New York 1988)

Hinrichs, D. M., *The Fateful Voyage of Captain Kidd* (New York, 1955)

Hoehling, A. A., *They Sailed Into Oblivion* (New York, 1957)

Hufton, G., and Baird, E., *Scarecrow's Legion* (Rochester, 1983)

Iron, John, Keeper of the Gate (London)

Kusche, L., *The Bermuda Triangle Mystery – Solved* (New York, 1975)

Lamont-Brown, Raymond, *Phantoms, Legends and Customs of the Sea* (London, 1972)

Lee, George Frederick, *Sights and Shadows* (London 1894)

Lockhart, J. G., *Mysteries of the Sea* (London, 1924)

Lord, Walter, *A Night to Remember* (New York, 1955)

Lowell, Thomas, *The Sea Devils' Fo'c's'le* (New York, 1929)

Lucie-Smith, Edward, *Outcasts of the Sea* (London, 1978)

Munro, D. T., *The Roaring Forties and After* (London)

O'Donnell, Elliott, *Haunted Waters* (London, 1957)

O'Donnell, Elliott, *Strange Sea Mysteries* (London, 1926)

Phillips, Ken, *Shipwrecks of the Isle of Wight* (Newton Abbot, 1988)

Robertson, Morgan, *The Wreck of the Titan* (Conn., USA 1981)

Robertson, Morgan and Stevenson, Ian, *The Wreck of the Titan: The Paranormal Experience Connected with the sinking of the Titanic* (Conn, 1974)

Rolt, L. T. C., *Isambard Kingdom Brunel* (London, 1957)

Sanderson, I., *Invisible Residents* (New York, 1970)

Saxon, L., *Lafitte the Pirate* (London and New York, 1930)

Shaw, F. H., *Famous Shipwrecks* (London, 1930)

Slocum, Joshua, *Sailing Alone Around the World* (New York, 1900)

Snow, E. R., *Mysterious Tales of the New England Coast* (New York, 1961)

Underwood, Peter, *Ghosts of Kent* (Rainham, Kent, 1984)

Verne, Jules, *A Floating City* (London, 1958)

Waugh, Mary, *Smuggling in Kent and Sussex*, 1700–1840 (Newbury, Berks, 1985)

Winer, Richard, *From the Devil's Triangle to the Devil's Jaw* (New York, 1974)

Winer, Richard, *The Devil's Triangle* (New York, 1974)

Notes And Sources

CHAPTER 1. Forewarned

A great number of books have been devoted to the *Titanic* and her fateful maiden voyage. In researching her associations with the paranormal I found Brown (1981), Beke (1986), Greenhouse (1971) and Robertson (1974) to be of particular value. In addition, a number of books, including Beesley (1912), Hoehling (1957) and Lord (1955) were used for general background information.

Beesley's account of the *Titanic* is particularly interesting. He was a survivor of the collision and rapidly got his memories into print. Although he makes no particular reference to the paranormal, he does make mention of a group of stokers who, due to lack of punctuality, were unable to board the vessel, arriving at her Southampton berth just as she was leaving. Almost certainly they were the brothers Slade and their fellow lodger Penney. In all, 22 of the ship's crew failed to report for duty.

A number of newspapers were employed in putting this chapter together, in particular these were as follows: *Southampton Times and Hampshire Express*, *Hampshire Independent*, *Belfast Evening Telegraph*, *Belfast Newsletter*, *New York Tribune*, *Montreal Star*, *Cork Examiner*, *Isle of Thanet Gazette* and *The Washington Post*.

CHAPTER 2. **Yo, Ho, Oh ... !**

Accounts of ghosts associated with Captain William Kidd, Jean Lafitte and Sapangani are all part of folk tradition. Little real evidence exists as to the sightings of these apparitions. Further references to these traditions may be found in Cohen (1984), Hadfield (1937) and Hallam (1977). More information about the lives of Lafitte and Kidd can be found in Lucie-Smith (1978) and Kidd is best treated by Hinrichs (1955) and Lafitte by Saxon (1930).

CHAPTER 3. **The Pilot of the *Pinta***

This entire account is based on Joshua Slocum's own narrative which appeared in his *Sailing Alone Around the World*. Of course, it could easily be suggested that the combination of an excessive intake of plums and white cheese might well lead to halucinations. Perhaps somebody reading this account might like to try Slocum's ill-advised meal in order to discover if a similar visitor makes an appearance!

CHAPTER 4. **The Ghost of the *Great Eastern***

A belief in the *Great Eastern* having been haunted goes back almost as far as her launch. However, actual evidence is limited. Reference to the ghost may be found in several books and these include Dugan (1953), Dumpleton (1982), Ellison (1955), Emmerson (1980), Lamont-Brown (1972), Rolt (1957), Verne (1958) and Winer (1974).

Contemporary newspapers examined were the *The Times*, the *New York Times* and *Scientific America*, together with local newspapers covering Birkenhead, London and Weymouth.

CHAPTER 5. **The Transparent Lady**

The main source for this chapter was Captain Alldridge's own account which appeared in the *Pembroke County Guardian* of February 16th 1901. In addition I confirmed parts of the story through use of the following material held at the Public Record Office (Kew): ADM180/14 (Progress Book) and ADM53/6239–6248 (Log Books). Unfortunately, no Muster Books could be located. These might have determined whether *Asp* had a high crew turnover as Alldridge states. Reference was also made to documents held in the Post Office Archives, London. Newspapers examined were the *The Times* and *Galloway Advertizer and Wigtonshire Free Press*.

CHAPTER 6. **A Malevolent Ghost**

Most of the information regarding the *St Paul* capsizing in the Hudson River was drawn from contemporary copies of the *New York Herald* and *New York Evening Post*. For the collision with HMS *Gladiator* use was again made of contemporary newspapers, including *The Times*, Portsmouth based *Hampshire Telegraph* and *Naval and Military Record*. Of additional value was Phillips (1988).

It is interesting to note that the *St Paul* might well be considered an unlucky ship. Apart from her collision with *Gladiator* and that subsequent accident off Pier 61, she also lost five of her crew when her main steam pipe burst in the engine room (1895), ran aground off New Jersey and was left in hazardous condition (1896), broke her starboard propellor in mid-Atlantic with the result that the racing engine wrecked four of her six cylinders (1900). Superstitious mariners have often been inclined to associate unlucky ships with difficult launchings. In March 1895, the *St Paul* failed to achieve a smooth launch, being stuck on her ways for a fortnight. Another unlucky ship, and one that suffered a similarly embarrassing launch, was Brunel's *Great Eastern*. It will be remembered from chapter four that she was stranded on the Thames mud banks for four months.

CHAPTER 7. **Phantom Ships**

The account of the *Khosuru/Tricolor* incident has been based on G. E. Robinson's own account which appeared in the June 1958 edition of the US Naval Institute's Proceedings under the title, *The Maimyo and the Tricoleur*. I have, however, reverted to the spelling of *Tricolor* as adopted by *Lloyd's List*. In addition I referred to Winer (1974) whose version of the incident, based I assume on Robinson's account, appears to be somewhat misleading. To supplement Robinson's article I also referred to various copies of *Lloyd's List*. These give full details of the movement of both *Tricolors* and of the loss of the first vessel to be given this name. Incidentally, it seems likely that Winer, in attempting to add excitement to the incident, may have missed something of even greater interest. There seems every possibility that the first *Tricolor* may have been deliberately destroyed. It appears that she may have been illegally running guns to the east and sunk by opponents of whatever cause they were intended for. Although her manifest did not indicate her to have been carrying weapons, several boxes of guns and ammunition were washed on to nearby beaches following the explosion. Unfortunately, papers relating to a secret inquiry were unavailable for examintion.

As regards the *Thresher* incident, this was drawn from Lamont-Brown (1972), but he fails to give an original source. I contacted the writer, but unfortunately he was only able to indicate that it came from the US Naval Academy, Annapolis. In writing to them I drew a blank. They were extremely helpful but were not able to locate the source.

Other books used in writing this chapter were de la Croix (1957) and Hadfield (1937).

CHAPTER 8. The *Ellen Austin* Mystery

The earliest account of the *Ellen Austin*'s encounter with a derelict ship in mid-Atlantic can be found in Gould (1944). Later accounts of this same incident appear in Gaddis (1965), Sanderson (1970), Lamont-Brown (1972), Berlitz (1974) and Winer (1974). Research into the origin of this mystery and research undertaken by Kusche can be found in Kusche (1975) and Hines (1988).

My own examination of the *Ellen Austin* mystery included the *The Times* index for 1881 together with *Lloyd's List* and the *Royal Gazette and Newfoundland Advertiser* for this same year.

It should be noted that, with approximately 2,000 vessels being lost at sea during that one year, research so far carried out into this particular derelict cannot be considered exhaustive.

CHAPTER 9. The Headless Mate

George Frederick Lee (1894), provides a basic account of the ill-omened *Squando*. However, he does not indicate an original source, although he frequently refers to the Norwegian consul resident in Bathurst. Elliott O'Donnell (1926) adds a few minor details. According to Lamont-Brown (1972), O'Donnell learnt of the incident while he was staying in the International Hotel, San Francisco. More likely however, O'Donnell got most of his information from George Frederick Lee's book, while adding a few pieces of his own in order to colour the story. Ideally, I would like to have verified details of the mate's murder, but I was unable to discover any further details.

CHAPTER 10. **The Legend of the Damned**

Full details of the voyage of Prince George may be found in 'The Cruise of His Majesty's Ship *Bacchante*, 1879–1882' and compiled from letters, journals and notebooks belonging to Prince George and his brother Prince Albert Victor. The quote concerning the supposed sighting of the Flying Dutchman is drawn from page 551 of Volume I. It should be noted that the future king was a midshipman on board HMS *Bacchante*, but had been temporarily transferred to HMS *Inconstant* while the *Bacchante* was being dry docked.

For information on the *General Grant* I drew considerable information from several contemporary newspapers, including the *Melbourne Leader* and the *Illustrated London News*. In addition, reference was made to Lamont-Brown (1972) and Eunson (1974).

CHAPTER 11. **The Ghost of *Eurydice***

An excellent account of the loss of HMS *Eurydice* may be found in Phillips (1988). My own research leaned heavily upon contemporary issues of the *The Times* and *The Hampshire Telegraph*. The record of the subsequent court martial held at the Public Record Office (ADM1/6474) was also referred to.

Details of the supernatural events surrounding the loss of *Eurydice* were gleaned from a variety of additional sources. In particular, I corresponded with Mrs E. Maleham, whose grandmother was Eleanor Bennett. The account of John MacNeill's premonition was drawn from Admiral Charles Beresford's autobiography [see Beresford (1914)].

CHAPTER 12. Smuggling Haunts

Most tales relating to one time smugglers haunting the coasts of England are based on hearsay. Tracking down any real evidence is virtually impossible.

Among books referred to for this chapter were a number of general accounts devoted to the subject of smuggling. Of particular value was Waugh (1985) and Hufton (1983). Only the latter makes any direct reference to folktales of smugglers who still haunt the area with which they were once associated. Of supernatural interest are Underwood (1984) and Hadfield (1937).

CHAPTER 13. Into the Teeth of Death

The traditional, but now discredited, 'Palatine' version of events may be found in Hadfield (1937), Lockhart (1924), Cohen (1989) and the Collected Works of J. G. Whittier.

For material relating to the re-assessment of this episode in the history of Block Island it is necessary to refer to the *Boston Gazette* (1739) and the *Boston Weekly News Letter* (1739) as well as the following more recently published items: Livermore, Rev., *History of Block Island* / Chapin, H. M., *The Discovery of the Real Palatine Ship* (Rhode Island Historical Society Collections Vol XVI:2, April 1923) / Kobler, John, *The Mystery of the Palatine Light* (Saturday Evening Post June 11th 1960)

CHAPTER 14. The Haunted Dockyard and other Naval Ghosts

Much of this chapter drew upon my own notes and correspondence. This was particularly the case with Chatham dockyard. I am grateful to the following for information on their own encounters with the supernatural world: Mrs M. A. Jarvis (the officers' terrace), Mr Samuel Arthur (Pembroke

Dock and Devonport), Mr Roy Davies (Pembroke Dock) and Mr L. S. Rockett (HMS *Mercury*). Additional help, as regards the ghost of Admiral Byng, was provided by the College Librarian, Royal Naval College, Greenwich.

As regards the ghost of Admiral Tryon, references may be found in Cohen (1989) and Winer (1974). The former I found to be a rather annoying book as it kept referring to Admiral Tryon as Admiral Tyrone, but there is no doubt it is Tryon to whom he refers! Melvin Harris's research into the Admiral Tryon apparition can be found in Harris (1986).

As well as being haunted, it was also claimed that the *Great Eastern* was a jinxed ship. In reality however, she was one of the safest ships to join the Atlantic run. Although she might roll violently, as in this severe storm encountered during 1861, her survival was never threatened.

Index

Aldington (Kent), 131, 137–140
Alldridge, Cmdr George Manley, 54–62, 185
America Line, 65
Atlantic Ocean, 147, 149
Aukland Islands, 113–9

Bathurst (New Brunswick), 99–102
Beesley, George, 135–7
Belfast, 15–16
Bellomont, Lord, 27, 28
Bennett, Able Seaman David Thomas, 127
Birkenhead, 51
Block Island (RI), 9, 143–161, 189
Boston (Mass), 27, 35, 96, 98, 100, 157
Brighton, 86
Bristol (RI), 40
Brook, Andrew, 148–151, 159
Brooklyn, 65
Brunel, Isambard Kingdom, 48
Butt, Major Archibald, 17, 23

Cape Cod, 84, 85
Cape Horn, 100, 112, 116
Cape of Good Hope, 106
Carter, George, 89
Ceylon (now Sri Lanka), 79–81
Chaleur Bay (New Brunswick), 84
Chatham Dockyard, 91, 93, 162–9, 189
Columbo, 79
Columbus, Christopher, 37, 40
Cuddiford, Able Seaman Benjamin, 126
Cunard Line, 68

Dee, River, 55, 60
Deptford, 41
Detroit, 19
Devonport, 168, 173
Dickens, Elizabeth, 157
Disappointment Island, 112
Donaghadee, 65
Dover, 43
Duff, David, 51–2

English Channel, 43, 70, 122–8, 147
Evans, Capt Walter, 49–50
Execution Dock, 28

Fairhaven, 35
Fayal, Isle of, 36
Fletcher, Ordinary Seaman Sidney, 126

'Flying Dutchman' legend, 103–119
Fokke, Capt Bernard, 106–7

Galveston (Texas), 31, 32, 33
Gardiner's Island, 27
General Post Office, 60
George, Prince (later King of Britain), 107
ghosts, passim
    explanation of, 7–8
Goodwin Sands, 89–93
Gould, Cmdr R. T. (author), 94
Greenwich, 175–6

Hadfield, R. L. (author), 154–6
Happisburgh, 141
Hare, Hon Marcus Augustus, 121, 124–8
Harrison, William, 48
Hastings, 45, 48, 53
Haverfordwest, 57
Hawkhurst, 131, 135–6
Hudson River, 66–7
Hurst Channel, 70

Ingoldsby Legends, 140

Jenkins, Capt Langworthy, 126

Keyham, 61
Kidd, Capt William, 24–28, 184
Krakatoa, 86

Lafitte, Jean, 30–32
Lamont-Brown, Raymond, (author), 117,
    184
Lipscombe, Cmdr F., 128
Livermore, Rev Samuel T., 156–7
Lizard, 88
Long Island, 24, 27
Lumsden, Capt Walter, 71, 73–5

Margate, 18
MacNeill, Sir John, 124, 129, 188
Marconi, Guglielmo, 69
Martyn Roads, 57
Mediterranean, 86
Melbourne, 112
Mercury, HMS, (naval establishment), 8,
    172–3, 190
Morgan, J. P., 20
Morvah, 141

Nelson, Admiral Horatio, 165, 178
Newfoundland, 96
New Orleans, 31
New York, 16, 27, 49, 63, 65–67, 96, 100
Nova Scotia, 84

Orinoco, 40
Orr's Island (Maine), 84
Oslo, 78

Palatine Light, legend of, 143–161
Passow, Capt Frederick, 69–72
Pembroke, 58–9, 174–5, 190
Pepys, Samuel, 166
Pico, Isle of, 36
pirates, 24–33
Portland, 70
Portpatrick, 60, 61
Portsmouth, 54–5, 70, 93, 127, 169–172

Queenstown, 14

Ramsgate, 89, 140, 145
Reculver, 134
Review of Reviews, 18, 180
riding officers, 131–140
Robertson, Morgan, 20–22
Robinson, G. E., 80
Romney Marsh, 133–5
Rotterdam, 82–3, 147
Russell, John Scott, 47–8

St Ives, 88
St John's (Newfoundland), 97
San Francisco, 84, 100
Sarangani, 29–30
Shepton Mallett, 141
ships
    Amherst (brig), 115
    Antonio (sloop), 27
    Asp, (naval paddle steamer), 54–62
    Bacchante (corvette), 188
    Camperdown (battleship), 177
    Cleopatra (corvette), 107, 109
    Ellen Austin (merchant sailing ship), 94–8,
        187
    Emma (schooner), 126
    Eurydice (naval sail training ship), 8, 9,
        121–9, 188
    General Grant (sailing ship), 111–119, 188
    George Washington (passenger liner), 16
    Gladiator (2nd class cruiser), 70–77, 185
    Inconstant (frigate), 107–8, 188
    Khosuru (freighter), 80–81, 82, 186
    Kobenhavn (sail training ship), 83–4
    Lady Lovibund (schooner), 89
    Monarch (third rate), 176

Montrose (passenger liner), 91
Neptune (sailing ship), 88
Nicholas (galley), 86
Northumberland (third rate), 91
Orkney Belle (whaler), 110–111
Packet Light (sailing ship), 84
Porthos (passenger liner), 79
Pinta (caravel), 37–9
Princess Augusta (merchant sailing ship),
    145–161
Quedah Merchant (sailing ship), 26–8
Raissonable (third rate), 165
Renown (second rate), 163
Restormel (collier), 68
St Paul (passenger liner), 64, 65–76, 185
Silvia Onorato (freighter), 90
Shrewsbury (third rate), 93
Somerset (trading vessel), 151
Spray (sloop), 34–40
Squando (barque), 90–102, 187
Temeraire (third rate), 163
Tennessee (clipper), 84
Terror (destroyer), 68
Thresher (submarine), 85–6, 87, 186
Titanic (passenger liner), 6, 10, 11–22,
    180, 183
Tourmaline (corvette), 107, 109
Tricdor (freighter), 78–82, 86, 186
Van Holt (cargo ship), 82–3
Victoria (battleship), 177–9
Victory (first rate), 163, 168
Violet (steam packet), 89
Warrior (battleship), 175
White Rover (sailing ship), 84
smugglers, 130–142, 189
Southampton, 12–15, 67–8, 69, 70, 74, 183

Thames, River, 41–2, 28
Thanet, Isle of, 18, 140
'Titan' (fictitious liner), 20–21
Tonbridge, 134
Tryon, Admiral Sir George, 177–180, 190

United States Naval Institute, 9

Vanderdecken, Capt Cornelius, 106, 107,
    117
Van der Line, Mary, 150–1, 156
Verne, Jules, 50

Wapping, 28
West Indies, 122
Weymouth, 42
Whitby, 141–2
White Star Company, 14, 20, 22, 68
Whittier, John Greenleaf (poet), 153–4, 189
Wight, Isle of, 69, 121, 123
Winer, Richard (author), 81
Wold, Capt Arthur, 78